THE ELEMENTARY SCHOOL
PRINCIPAL'S
CALENDAR

To our families—for their love and support

To our students—our hope for the future

*To our colleagues—who gave us the gift
of their professional practices*

THE ELEMENTARY SCHOOL
PRINCIPAL'S
CALENDAR

A MONTH-BY-MONTH PLANNER
FOR THE SCHOOL YEAR

ROBERT RICKEN • MICHAEL TERC • IDA AYRES

CORWIN PRESS, INC.
A Sage Publications Company
Thousand Oaks, California

For information:

Corwin Press, Inc.
A Sage Publications Company
2455 Teller Road
Thousand Oaks, California 91320
E-mail: order@corwinpress.com

Sage Publications Ltd.
6 Bonhill Street
London EC2A 4PU
United Kingdom

Sage Publications India Pvt. Ltd.
M-32 Market
Greater Kailash I
New Delhi 110 048 India

Printed in the United States of America

Library of Congress Cataloging-in-Publication Data

Ricken, Robert.
    The elementary school principal's calendar: A month-by-month planner
for the school year / by Robert Ricken, Michael Terc, and Ida Ayres.
        p.   cm.
    ISBN 0-7619-7827-5 (cloth: acid-free paper)
    ISBN 0-7619-7828-3 (pbk.: acid-free paper)
        1. Schedules, School—United States—Handbooks, manuals, etc.
    2. Elementary school principals—United States—Handbooks, manuals, etc.
    I. Terc, Michael. II. Ayres, Ida. III. Title.
    LB3032 .R54   2001
    372. 12'012—dc21   00-012765

This book is printed on acid-free paper.

01 02 03 04 05 06 07 7 6 5 4 3 2 1

Aquisition Editor: Robb Clouse
Editorial Assistant: Kylee Liegl
Production Editor: Denise Santoyo
Editorial Assistant: Kathryn Journey
Designer/Typesetter: Marion Warren/Lynn Miyata
Cover Designer: Michelle Lee

Contents

Resources

Preface

---

*T*he National Association of Elementary School Principals identified four fundamental areas that are prerequisites for success as a principal:

1. *Advanced understanding of the teaching and learning process.* A school leader must be solidly grounded in both contemporary and traditional instructional techniques. There is a need in schools for a blend of both. Principals must be able to recognize effective teaching, evaluate progress in learning, and demonstrate commitment to enhancing learning for all students, regardless of their socioeconomic background or ability.

2. *A thorough understanding of child growth and development and of adult learning.* School leaders must have expert knowledge in the field of child growth and development as well as experience in teaching children. They must be capable of ensuring that the curriculum is both challenging and developmentally appropriate. To work effectively in the area of professional development, a school leader must understand how adults learn, their readiness to change, their interpersonal relationship styles, and their receptiveness to making choices about their learning.

3. *A broad base of knowledge, including a solid background in the liberal arts.* A school leader must have some kind of liberal arts foundation that provides a firm grasp of basic curriculum content and an understanding of the relationship between that body of knowledge and the elementary and middle-level curriculum.

4. *A sincere commitment to educational equity and excellence at all levels for children.* A school leader must be a caring person who knows how to create a learning climate that is based on mutual trust and respect, that produces high morale, and that places high emphasis on the fact that all students can succeed.

In the contemporary American elementary school, we believe the attributes listed above must be combined with a sincere understanding and belief in the concept of being a leader of leaders. Viewing our staff as partners from the planning process through the implementation stage must augment the values professed by the National Association of Elementary School Principals. The team concept is no longer a lofty ideal. It is a basic tenet of our profession.

Our book stresses the "nuts and bolts" of the principal's responsibilities. We believe that highly intelligent administrators often fail because of their lack of organizational skills. Nothing demoralizes a staff more than canceled meetings, postponed teacher observations, and surprises that negate their instructional plans. (We are not minimizing the characteristics stated above.) However, staff confidence in the principal is also earned by the calm, orderly tone of the building's day-to-day operational mode. This book is a gift of our experience. We are pleased to share these practices with you. We hope you add many items to your own repertoire, and we invite you to send examples of your own practices to us to include them in our next edition.

About the Authors

Robert Ricken, EdD, served as a junior high school principal and school superintendent in the Mineola School District in New York and has been an interim superintendent in New York's North Bellmore, Smithtown, Elmont, Half Hollow Hills, and Bellmore-Merrick Central high school districts. He was the Long Island Coordinator for the Anti-Defamation League's "A World of Difference Institute," and he has conducted antibias workshops and inservice programs in over 100 school districts. He presently teaches educational administration at Long Island University, C. W. Post Campus. He is the author of *Love Me When I'm Most Unlovable . . . The Middle School Years, Book Two: The Kids' View; The RA Guide to Nassau County Schools; Middle School Calendar: A Handbook for Practitioners;* and *The High School Principal's Calendar.* He has been published in *The New York Times, Newsday, Sports Illustrated, The Harvard Review, Harper's Weekly, Single Parent Magazine, The National Association of Secondary School Principals' Journal, The School Administrator, Long Island Magazine, New York State School Board Journal,* and many other professional magazines. He has been designated the Administrator of the Year by Phi Delta Kappa of Hofstra University and the Administrator of the Year by the Nassau-Suffolk Educators' Association; he has also been recognized for his work in labor relations by the New York State Council of Administrators and Supervisors. He received the Award of Honor for his outstanding contributions to education through his exemplary public relations practices from the National Public Relations Association. In 1992 he received the Outstanding Service Support Award from the Girl Scouts of Nassau County, and in 1994 he received the Dr. Martin Luther King, Jr., Recognition Award. Recently he was recognized by the board of directors of the New York State Middle School Association with the Ross M. Burkhardt Middle Level Educator Award in recognition for his promotion of middle-level education.

Michael Terc, MA, PD, is an administrator in the Mineola Public School District. For the last 16 years, he has served as assistant principal at Mineola High School, Mineola, New York. Before this, he taught mathematics at Mineola Middle School for 16 years. He also served as principal of the Mineola Summer School Program for two years. During his career, he has coached many sports and has been involved in a host of student activities. He served as president of the Nassau County Baseball Coaches Association and in 1976 was selected as the *Daily News' High School Baseball Coach of the Year.* In 1982 he authored "Coordinate Geometry and Art: A Match," published in *National Council of Mathematics Teachers Journal.* In 1994 he received the Jenkins Service Award, the highest service award given by the Mineola School District's PTA Association. He received his MA in mathematics from Hofstra University and was awarded a Professional Diploma in educational administration from Long Island University, C. W. Post Campus. He recently was selected by the School Administrators Association of New York State to receive its 1999-2000 New York State Distinguished Assistant Principal of the Year Award. His most recent publication was *The High School Principal's Calendar.*

Ida Ayres, MA, is the principal of a 550-student elementary school in Mineola, New York. Prior to coming to Mineola, she taught in a Westchester parochial school for five years and then continued her career as a learning disabilities teacher for a New Rochelle, New York, public school. She was awarded the principalship of a large parochial elementary school in New Rochelle, becoming one of the first lay principals at a parochial school in New York. During her tenure, she established a middle school concept and brought the school to statewide recognition for the effective use of individualized instruction. She also taught at St. John's University for one year. However, the passion to lead children, teachers, and parents brought her back to her roots—elementary education. The following year she was appointed the principal of the Jackson Avenue School in Mineola. In that role, Mrs. Ayres and her staff have successfully implemented many new concepts, including parallel block scheduling, a plan for professional development whereby classroom teachers meet with school specialists on a weekly basis for purposes of integrating curriculum; an exciting site-based management team initiative designed to involve all parents, particularly non-English-speaking parents, in the education of their children; and a Chapter 1-ESL partnership. She has made presentations for the Nassau County Elementary Principals, ESL conference, and local professional meetings, and she has received honorable mention for excellence in educational administration from the School Administrators Association of New York State. She holds a master's degree from the College of New Rochelle and has completed most of her doctoral work at Columbia University.

Chapter One

Are You a Leader or a Boss?

The Boss drives his people; the Leader coaches his.
The Boss uses authority, the Leader wins goodwill.
The Boss keeps them guessing; the Leader arouses their enthusiasm.
The Boss talks about "I"; the Leader makes it "We."
The Boss makes work drudgery; the Leader makes work a game.
The Boss says, "Go"; the Leader says, "Let's go."
—Ted Pollock

Principals who are employed for a 10-month school year are simply guaranteeing the district that they will work during their summer vacation. It is impossible to leave in June and return a few days prior to the opening of the new school year with a sense of confidence. The planning we do in the summer ensures a smooth and organized school opening. Efficiency is not an accident. If everything operates like clockwork, principals have put in the necessary extra time. If the tone of the building is calm and teachers are confident and in control, it's because we've addressed the numerous behind-the-scenes tasks. Lao-Tsu has said, "The great leader is he who the people say, we did it ourselves." Our self-satisfaction comes from the knowledge that our attention to detail created the orderly environment that will set a positive tone for our academic year.

Whenever we finish reading a book, we close the cover and mentally review the experience. This is exactly what principals do in the beginning of July. We evaluate the past year, reviewing our successes, developing strategies to improve every aspect of our school's operations, and, more significantly, assessing our own professional practices as well.

In a sense, the "book" remains slightly open as we complete the review of the past year and determine our goals for the future. Many of our decisions will be predicated upon the performance reviews of our teachers and students. This evaluation is a minimal expectation for the dedicated principal. As a truly dedicated leader we must be a V.I.P.—not a Very Important Person, but rather a **V**isionary with **I**ntegrity and a **P**assionate advocate for our school, staff, and students.

In the present era, our planning process should involve the entire school community. Staff members will be unable to maintain a collective vision for the future unless they are part of our action plan. Each year we should be reaching for a higher level of professional practice. This can be accomplished only through honest and open evaluations and by developing new objectives stressing these elevated expectations. If you coast, you can only go downhill. The dynamic energy of the principal creates a pressure to improve. The status quo must go!

We are responsible for creating a framework for success. The development of this "charged" atmosphere comes from us. Staff members will become believers when we give them evidence that caring is an action word.

The "nuts and bolts" delineated in each monthly chapter are our professional responsibility. We set the tone in order to free our staff to become more creative and to be the driving force in implementing our collective plans.

The joys and satisfactions of the end of one year are often replaced by the sudden silence, tranquility, and loneliness of an empty building. July's struggle is akin to changing gears. The lethargy has to be reversed and replaced by a renewal of energy. Taking vacation time or attending a conference may help the principal to make this adjustment.

July's Key Tasks

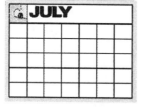

✳ *Summer School*

Just a few years ago, elementary summer schools were more like day camps than a support system for raising academic standards. Today, with an emphasis on increased state mandates, summer schools focus on remediation and enrichment activities. Elementary principals would be wise to:

1. Take an active role in developing the summer school program

2. Make certain that the summer school principal or teacher-in-charge understands the enhanced academic mission of the school

3. Help set the rules for behavior, particularly if the school is housed in your building

4. Provide for a means to share student progress with your full-time staff members

Summer school was once viewed as a frill. Today it is an excellent means to enhance the results of the regular school year.

Personal Commentary/Notes: _____

_____

Curriculum-Writing Projects ✳

Many districts pay faculty to revise or create curriculum over the summer. These projects should be supervised by an elementary school administrator or the chair of the appropriate department. Their role is to ensure that the staff is performing the tasks outlined in the curriculum-writing proposal. If the summer writers stay on task, their final product will help classroom teachers to be more efficient and to upgrade their skills.

These writers must adhere to timelines in order for the finished product to reach the teachers at the start of the school year. Too often, the duplication of the final project is delayed. This is an occasion when a principal's demands should be nonnegotiable.

Personal Commentary/Notes: _____

_____

Review Teacher Evaluations ✳

The hectic pace of the school year usually makes it impossible for the principal to review the folders of the entire staff. The time is often used to target several teachers whose performance needs improvement or who are new to the building or profession. The summer lull is an appropriate time to read each staff folder and prepare input for your administrative team.

Every teacher should have some specific goals for the upcoming year. Often we neglect experienced teachers. They, too, need a "pat on the back" via a personal note, along with ideas for them to share their expertise. Mentoring new staff members, teaching model lessons, and joining curriculum-writing teams are appropriate activities to involve experienced teachers. We believe that part of the June final evaluation should be some form of goal setting for the upcoming September. Supervision should be an ongoing process.

Personal Commentary/Notes: _____

_____

✳ Meeting With Custodial Staff

Meeting with the head custodian and the supervisor of buildings and grounds is a must. We believe every one of these staff members should be evaluated as is done with the professional staff. When custodians begin to be less effective, the entire building suffers. They are part of the team and should view themselves as members of the elementary school staff.

Second on the agenda is a thorough review of the summer custodial work schedule. New budgets often target projects, and the principal should set the parameters with the buildings and grounds administrators. Special projects that were funded in the budget, if completed effectively, demonstrate to board members and staff that the budget-building process is worth the time, energy, and effort.

A careful check of all equipment associated with the playground area is a must. Conducting such a walk-through with the head custodian should ensure a safe environment. Keep a record of your findings on file, and conduct periodic checks throughout the year to make sure that small problems are fixed in a timely manner. The adage "an ounce of prevention is worth a pound of cure" certainly applies in this instance.

*Personal Commentary/Notes:*_____

_____

✳ Review and Revise the Student Handbook

With computers, the process of revising the student handbook is more manageable. Most administrators maintain files on almost everything they do during the year. An assistant principal in a New York school district informed us that she drops little notes into a file titled "Student Handbook," noting revisions or ideas for the upcoming year. In July, she reviews each new idea with the principal and later reproduces the revised handbook.

In one year, she included a wording change in the school's mission statement; a board policy statement in regard to the disciplinary code; an updated list of clubs, advisers, and new staff members; and new requirements for Student Council.

*Personal Commentary/Notes:*_____

_____

✳ Update Teacher Handbook

We believe the involvement of a small group of teachers in this process is essential. It is an excellent activity for one or two of our experienced staff members. Who knows better than they do what teachers need in a handbook? Ideally, the principal (or his or her designee) will merely have to implement the teachers' suggestions during the summer. As part of its orientation program, a district in

Texas has new teachers evaluate the handbook anonymously. In this way, the principal secures input from new faculty members who often have experience from other settings.

It's important for newly hired teachers to familiarize themselves with the specific rules and procedures of a new school before they enter the building in the fall. Therefore, try to give them copies of the manual in August. Receiving it on the first day of school can be intimidating and doesn't allow the new teacher time to digest the material and to ask questions. (See Resource A—Teacher Handbook.)

Personal Commentary/Notes: _____

_____

Review Policy Manual ✳

This task is easily overlooked during the academic year. The principal should review both building and board policies, with special attention given to new or revised policies. The effects of items such as new requirements, new state mandates, changes in child abuse reporting regulations, Megan's law notification, smoke-free environments, new curricula, and the disciplinary code are examples of changes that may require a meeting with the superintendent.

Personal Commentary/Notes: _____

_____

Develop a Mission Statement ✳

A formal, written mission statement should be in place before any school improvement efforts are undertaken. This helps avoid a haphazard approach to school improvement in which numerous, sometimes conflicting efforts occur simultaneously and the staff members are drained of vital energy and motivation. (See Resource B—How to Build a Mission Statement.)

Personal Commentary/Notes: _____

_____

Review and Revise Administrative Responsibilities ✳

We are all frequently married to tradition. The superintendent of schools has a table of organization for the district. A thorough analysis of the staff and line responsibilities of each administrator ensures that every person and subject area are being appropriately supervised. Shifts in responsibility can be made to improve supervision, to adjust workloads, or to conform with revised state mandates and laws. With frequent budget shortfalls, the principal would be wise to plan for a reduction in staff and how it would have the least effect on the building's table of organization.

*Personal Commentary/Notes:*_____

_____

✳ *Attend Monthly Board Meetings*

Board of education meetings are the elementary school principal's opportunity to publicly review the achievements of his students and staff. Having just attended all of the closing events and the graduation or moving-up exercises, it is important to transfer that joy and enthusiasm to the board and community. It is an awesome public relations opportunity. Reducing this report to writing and having it published in the local newspaper or in the school district newsletter is vital in securing community support for the elementary school. The authors view this as a critical segment of a principal's public relations plan.

*Personal Commentary/Notes:*_____

_____

✳ *Trend Analysis of Disciplinary Referrals*

Disciplinary trends should be monitored throughout the year, but an annual study is necessary to fully assess the schoolwide program. We suggest the following:

1. Compare numbers of referrals with those of the previous year.

2. Put referrals into categories, such as misbehavior in class, playground, cafeteria, buses, and so forth.

3. Itemize by teacher.

4. Itemize by grade level.

A July roundtable discussion of the data should be held with the building principal and the key staff members in charge of discipline. Significant data should be reviewed and, if necessary, procedures adjusted. Sometimes, individual teachers or aides are submitting an extraordinary number of referrals. The principal should assist those staff members to develop more effective disciplinary techniques.

*Personal Commentary/Notes:*_____

_____

Examine School Statistics ✻

Data such as the number of students at or above grade-level expectations should be examined. The principal should review standardized test results and year-end grades. Significant changes and trends should be reflected in school-wide goals for the upcoming school year. Trends should be discussed with staff and district curriculum supervisors. Where necessary, inservice courses should be developed to target areas in need of improvement. These courses should also assist teachers with learning any new skills required to address increased emphasis on higher academic standards.

Personal Commentary/Notes: _____

_____

Assess Each Grade Level ✻

A meeting should be held with each grade-level leader to review curriculum changes, personnel issues, and goals for the coming year. This session usually "flags" potential problems for the principal to address.

Personal Commentary/Notes: _____

_____

Hold Meetings With Parents ✻

We believe in the ongoing value of meetings between the elementary school principal and the parents of his or her students. These informal but regular contacts with parents are an essential and useful activity. The principal can also invite other members of the staff to these meetings to discuss a host of topics to keep parents informed about their child's adjustment and academic programs. Health issues and child development concerns may also provide information, offer suggestions, and reduce tensions. These meetings frequently defuse potential controversial issues. They also afford the principal a pipeline to community feelings about his or her school activities and staff.

Personal Commentary/Notes: _____

_____

Calendar ✻

The elementary school principal should review the school district calendar for the upcoming academic year. Only those dates that are exclusively elementary school priorities should be included in the district calendar. Events such as graduation, school plays, report cards, testing dates, PTA meetings, field day, science fairs, concerts, and parent-teacher conferences are a few examples of pertinent items. Proposed dates should be discussed with other elementary principals and the middle school and high school principals. This is particularly important when certain elementary school events require the use of the secondary school auditoriums.

The elementary school calendar must be coordinated by the principal and his or her secretary. Take special care to avoid scheduling activities on religious holidays. The plethora of events at any elementary school should not conflict with other school district activities. This skill is akin to that of the person who develops the master schedule. You simply cannot publish a calendar and then realize that you have conflicts. Scheduling two events at the same time or scheduling an activity that interrupts the educational program causes the staff and community to lose confidence in their management team. Use the past year as a guide and be certain that requests for changes do not have a negative effect on another club or event. This is one of the rare times when a degree of rigidity is a virtue.

*Personal Commentary/Notes:*_____

_____

July's Communications

∗ Letters to Staff

We believe the elementary school principal should write a letter of thanks to the faculty for their work during the past school year. The principal should include the highlights he or she mentioned in the presentation to the board of education. The letter should be a source of pride for the staff, especially when many faculty and student achievements are noted.

Including some information about the summer curriculum projects demonstrates that even during the vacation period, the elementary school is a work in progress. An update on construction projects, painting, and new equipment acquisition is also appreciated.

The next correspondence will probably be a welcome-back letter. As the summer begins, the staff deserves the accolades for past performances and the principal's best wishes.

*Personal Commentary/Notes:*_____

_____

Letter to the Incoming Kindergarten Class *

A letter of welcome is the principal's way of reaching out to the kindergarteners and their parents. This letter is a necessary early notification that serves many institutional, as well as student, needs. Most children have a high degree of anxiety as they await the start of school. This letter lets the kindergarteners know that you are preparing for their arrival and want to make their transition as comfortable as possible. It is equally important to include private and parochial students in this mailing, because they often have the additional fear of being forgotten or overlooked.

This letter should set forth the orientation dates and arrival times. In order to have a smooth school opening, the principal should mention the role of parents in helping to reduce anxiety. We should encourage and welcome calls from parents and guardians, because this may be a traumatic time for them as well.

Personal Commentary/Notes: _____

_____

Letters to New Staff *

No, we should not wait until the end of August to welcome our new staff and begin their orientation program. Many principals invite new teachers in during the summer for an informal chat and to pick up textbooks, curriculum guides, and faculty handbooks. It is a personal touch and a thoughtful way to reach out to new personnel.

The letter usually outlines the orientation process. Some districts not only bring in new teachers early but also have additional orientation and inservice sessions throughout the school year. Every item in the student and faculty handbook is appropriate. In many districts, a business official hosts a meeting to discuss payroll dates, health insurance, social security, and payroll deductions. Union officials may be invited in to discuss the teacher contract. This is usually separate from the formal district orientation.

Most of all, the letter is an invitation to join the school's family and the profession. Many schools assign new teachers to mentors to let them know they will have a confidante when the orientation process is fully operational. A compassionate letter with a hearty welcome is Phase 1 of the new teacher's orientation process.

Personal Commentary/Notes: _____

_____

Contact Your Local Police and Fire Officials *

Every school should have current disaster plans in the event of an emergency. Unfortunately, in contemporary America, violence, bomb threats, fire, and civil disturbances should be anticipated. In consultation with local law enforcement officers and school attorneys, the principal should learn his or her rights and responsibilities on a yearly basis, because school law and local statutes change frequently. For example, in New York State, the principal may resume classes after searching a building during a bomb scare. However, once the building is emptied and police are called in, the students may not reenter without police (not the school principal's) approval. Good relations are helpful during these troubled and uncertain emergency situations. In this "Catch-22" environment, caution is the watchword. Police professionalism should be respected, but the in loco parentis role of the principal is paramount. They are, in the final analysis, our children.

Fire officials should be given equal time. Most state education departments require a specific number of fire drills a year. Most insist upon a dozen, with approximately eight performed prior to December 31. Fire officials may check alarm boxes and discuss response time in emergency situations. Principals should be aware that in a fire, casualties are dramatically increased if students take longer than two minutes to exit a building.

Such meetings foster good relations with two of the community's most important service organizations. In most rural and suburban districts, the fire personnel are usually volunteers and are often your students' older siblings and parents.

Particularly in elementary schools, police and fire personnel visit classrooms to explain their jobs and to help discuss safety issues. Many field trips are scheduled to police stations and fire departments. School classes frequently participate in fire prevention and safety awareness poster contests. This is another example of building school-community cooperation.

*Personal Commentary/Notes:*_____

_____

✳ *Membership in Civic Associations*

Principals should consider joining groups such as Rotary, Lions, Kiwanis, and the Chamber of Commerce. The benefits are obvious. Membership provides support for elementary school activities, and principals are in turn able to present information about their students and staff to members of these prestigious organizations. Joining all clubs is not always practical. Thus, the decision should be evaluated annually.

A possible strategy is to allow assistant principals or staff members to join other local organizations to increase the school's involvement in such public relations efforts. The members of these service organizations are key communicators in the community. Their involvement often translates into a positive information flow to your residents.

*Personal Commentary/Notes:*_____

_____

Subscribe to Local Newspapers ✳

Being aware of local politics and community developments is vital. The letters to the editor section and civic newsletters provide a rich source of information. In addition, sending news releases on awards, honor roll lists, and school activities is another way to inform your public. This two-way flow of information benefits everyone. We have found that local newspapers provide more thorough elementary school coverage than major newspapers. The principal and PTA president should forward articles to the local community newspapers. The PTA should have meeting notices and descriptions of programs sent regularly to the newspapers.

Personal Commentary/Notes: _____

_____

Public Relations Program ✳

A written public relations program has all of the desired outcomes we have mentioned in the previous two tasks. Some districts have developed rather sophisticated public relations programs. A principal from Indiana sent us the following list in response to our query about his program:

1. School awards night
2. Student handbook
3. Open School Day and Open School Night
4. Picture day
5. Letters to parents
6. Book fairs
7. Grandparents/guardian day
8. Music concerts
9. Drama performances
10. School newspaper
11. PTA meetings
12. Board of Education presentations
13. Science fairs

Public relations, as you can see, is a broad-based, multifaceted approach to building community understanding and support for the complete array of activities going on within the elementary school. More is usually better!

Personal Commentary/Notes: _____

_____

July's Planning

* *Planning Trips by
School Organizations
and Fundraising Activities*

Our purpose is to develop a conflict-free calendar. Annual trips taken by classes should not be planned when there are potential conflicts. As our activities expand, conflicts even arise during the summer. A principal in Wisconsin mentioned his dilemma when a summer music camp was scheduled during the same week in August when the community had a major event. There were students who wanted to be involved in both activities. Thus our planning should not contribute to this dilemma.

With the increase of elementary summer school programs and day camp participation, the potential for conflict has increased. Maintaining a day-to-day calendar is now essential to avoid conflicts.

One assistant principal in New York created a fund-raising schedule to avoid misunderstandings between school groups over sale dates and the specific items to be marketed. What was once a cause of discontent is now a mutually agreed-upon standardized practice.

*Personal Commentary/Notes:*_____

_____

July's Personnel

* *Personnel*

The finalization of all faculty positions should be monitored. Any opening should be posted and advertised, and arrangements should be made for summer interviews. This process should be followed for all support staff as well.

We believe that all cocurricular positions should also be filled as early as possible. This contributes to a smooth opening for these activities in September. Ideally, club advisers will be able to plan during the summer.

A final check should also be made of contractual obligations. Timelines should be followed for staff who are scheduled for appointment to tenure. A similar review should be made for the nonteaching staff, particularly in states where they are governed by civil service law. They, too, have a form of tenure after a brief probationary period.

*Personal Commentary/Notes:*_____

_____

July's Checklists

July's Key Tasks and Reminders

Major Assignments	Date Started	Date Completed	Days on Task
Monitor summer school			
Review curriculum-writing projects			
Review teacher evaluations			
Meet with custodial staff			
Review and revise student handbook			
Review and revise teacher handbook			
Review school board's policy manual			
Develop a mission statement			
Review and revise administrative responsibilities			
Attend monthly board of education meetings			
Analyze trends in disciplinary referrals			
Examine school statistics			
Assess each grade level's status			
Hold meetings with parents			
Review school calendar for upcoming year			

July's Communications Checklist

✔	Assignment
	Write letter to staff
	Write letter to incoming kindergarten class
	Write letter to new staff members
	Establish contact with local police and fire department officials
	Establish membership in civic associations
	Subscribe to local newspapers
	Develop a public relations program

July's Planning Checklist

✔	Assignment
	Finalize calendar for field trips and fund-raising activities

July's Personnel Checklist

✔	Finalize
	Faculty positions and teaching schedules

JULY CALENDAR

MONTH: JULY

YEAR: _____

MONDAY	TUESDAY	WEDNESDAY	THURSDAY	FRIDAY	SATURDAY / SUNDAY

Notes: _____

Chapter Two

Do You Impart These Expectations to Your Staff?

My Ideal School

I believe our schools ought to be like
Harvard—with a strong academic curriculum
Like West Point—with excellent discipline
Like Disneyland—with organized, positive excitement for children.

—John H. Childs

*A*ugust is the transition from summer to the new school year. It is a return to an action mode. Each item on your to-do list, if properly addressed, will help provide a smooth opening of school. Although not every state begins the school year in September, the ideas and strategies are generally applicable.

Processing the information you discovered while meeting with key staff members over the past two months should provide the current data necessary for setting realistic future goals. It is clearly the time to formulate plans to help provide a clear focus for the coming months. Today, most schools involve the community as well as the staff in this goal-setting process. School improvement teams and site-based councils help to foster ownership and mobilize constituent groups to assist in achieving these new goals.

We believe the principal should establish personal goals as well. This task is left to you. However, when we examine why most principals have difficulty in achieving their own personal agenda, we find that the day-to-day pressures of the job often make self-reflection impossible. How can one look within when the to-do list is always full? A word about time management is appropriate, because it ultimately determines how effectively we plan our day and execute our priorities. The National Association of Secondary School Principals Department of Student Activities provides the following valuable time-management tips:

1. Pinpoint the time of day when you are most productive. Make the most of it.

2. Eliminate distractions in prime time.

3. Schedule high-priority, tough, and ugly jobs for prime hours.

4. Schedule easier, more interesting tasks for off-peak times.

5. Give low-priority tasks less attention.

6. Eliminate unimportant activities.

7. Make decisions now.

8. Make more realistic estimates of the time needed to complete a task.

9. Set priorities among jobs to do each day.

10. Break tasks into manageable sections.

11. Set deadlines for each section.

12. Finish tasks before starting new ones.

13. Delegate jobs that can be done by others.

14. Eliminate excessive paperwork.

15. Limit conversations to important items.

16. Pace your work to get results within a reasonable period of time.

17. Schedule breaks or changes in routine to avoid fatigue.

18. Limit your work hours each week.

19. Work while others are at lunch; eat earlier or later than others.

20. Arrive at appointments on time by listing when you have to leave, not the time of the appointment.

21. Have only one project on the desk at a time, the one you are currently working on.

22. Ask for information when you do not understand or when you need more facts.

23. Keep communication lines open.

24. Train staff members for new tasks.

25. Anticipate changes; prepare for them.

26. Confine conflicts to issues, not personalities.

Ideally, this list will provide one or more hints to enable each principal to maximize constructive time. This consideration is similar to our classroom suggestions to staff members, which are designed to enable them to reduce noninstructional time and maximize the teaching of the daily lesson.

Although many of the tasks can be reduced to a checklist, we believe a conscientious principal will be able both to involve staff members in the execution of these jobs and also to do much to humanize the school's educational environment. We asked principals throughout the United States how they involved their educational community in the summer while they worked alone to ready their school for the coming year. Their answers and techniques were varied, and we hope that some of these items will be meaningful to you and will perhaps add an idea or two to your professional repertoire.

A principal from Virginia asks her secretary to put the names and phone numbers of two of her teachers on her desk each day she works in the summer. The principal puts in a call to "touch base" with all of her staff members in this manner. The teachers are pleased she called, and many volunteer to assist with some of the school opening tasks. This is particularly valuable because so many of us do not have assistant principals.

One principal from California meets twice with his PTA during the summer. The first time is to finalize the topics and dates for PTA meetings, and the second time is to meet with parents who would like to volunteer during the school year. These parents have made welcome-back signs for the staff, have helped the secretary to box material for teachers, have drawn plans for improving the appearance of the outside of the building, and have developed plans for upgrading the school playgrounds.

A principal from Las Vegas, Nevada, has been faced with the problem of having many new residents register each year. She meets three days and one night each summer with new parents. These meetings are advertised in the local press. The sessions not only provide parents with an orientation to the school but also help to minimize first-day enrollment surprises. The evening session is provided because in many of her students' homes, both parents are employed and can't attend during the day.

A Vermont principal invites parents who are very concerned about their child's initial adjustment to kindergarten to come in one morning a week. They meet the principal and his secretary and take a walking tour of the building. She believes this helps to reduce the fear of the first school experience for the child and the parent who are having separation anxiety.

A principal from Long Island, New York, invites each team of grade-level teachers to have lunch with her while she works in the summer. The meetings must be voluntary because their union contract prohibits work without remuneration. She reports that teachers readily come in, unless they are away, and that many staff members are pleased to volunteer to assist with such things as distributing books, mentoring new teachers, becoming liaisons to the PTA, and serving on school or district committees. Another New York principal meets with his student leaders and reviews student council projects, safety squad assignments, and assembly honor guard formations. Although the summer is a quiet time, we believe that all the things accomplished in August reduce the workload throughout the year.

August's Key Tasks

Prepare School Opening *
Remarks for Staff

We perceive this welcome-back speech as one of the principal's important lesson plans. Similar to any teacher lesson we evaluate, all of the component parts should be included. Too many principals talk off the cuff and do not focus their remarks. This informal greeting falls short of the law in certain states where items such as disciplinary codes, child abuse guidelines, and emergency situations must be mentioned in a formal setting.

The scope of this presentation is limitless. Professors of educational administration frequently give their students this final examination question: Write your school opening speech for your first conference day held just prior to the start of school. We provide some critical components in the list below, though we are aware that you will delete some and add many of your own as you prepare for the new academic year.

1. Give thanks for past efforts.

2. Express hope that the well-deserved rest served as an energy renewal for the new year.

3. Introduce mentors and let them introduce new staff members' accomplishments and background. Principals may wish to do the honors themselves.

4. Review summer projects and accomplishments.

5. Discuss summer school and mention how the staff attempted to support the work of our regular classroom teachers.

6. Give legal data (if required). For example, in New York State any mention of child abuse must be reported, whether substantiated or not! Megan's Law is at a different status in each state (know yours!).

7. Read building's mission statement as an inspirational theme.

8. Discuss getting started:
   a. Review disciplinary code
   b. Highlight some teacher handbook items
   c. Suggest some first-day class expectations
   d. Review particular concerns for kindergarten students

9. Highlight the first class:
   a. Take attendance
   b. Discuss absence notes
   c. Discuss classroom rules
   d. Inform students about the supplies they will need
   e. Give homework, even if it is just to cover books and purchase supplies

10. Outline teacher responsibilities, including:
    a. Attendance procedures
    b. Lesson plans
    c. Grading procedures
    d. Sign in/out procedures
    e. Building assignment/duty periods

*Personal Commentary/Notes:*_____

_____

✳ *Meet With All Supervisors and Teachers-In-Charge*

These are key members of your school team. It makes sense to secure their input for your opening day remarks. In the process, you may be able to emphasize areas they will be discussing later with their grade levels, and also they may broaden your perspective and vision about your initial faculty meeting. By discussing how to motivate your entire faculty, you will also be demonstrating your expectations for your school staff leaders.

This is also your last chance to discover if there are any urgent needs at the department or classroom level. Each supervisor or teacher leader should be able to report on the readiness of his or her own department or grade level. Obviously, there is an unspoken expectation that these leaders have visited every classroom and talked with all of their classroom teachers. The principal must complete this task if there is no person to whom to delegate this assignment.

It is also the appropriate time to review the goals of each supervisor, the supervisors' departments, and their supervisory objectives for individual teachers. Ideally, this will be a review of what was discussed in June when you closed the books on the previous school year. This process ensures an orderly transition and a coherent supervisory process. Many elementary principals do not have assistant principals or supervisory staff. In such a case, everything becomes the principal's responsibility.

*Personal Commentary/Notes:*_____

_____

Board Presentation (if required)   *

Some districts require a board presentation by each principal prior to the start of school. If this is required, the principal has the perfect opportunity to present the accomplishments of the past and the goals for the coming year. Involving the staff in the preparation of the speech serves as a reminder of the recent progress made by the teachers and is often a major boost to staff morale.

Personal Commentary/Notes: _____

_____

Set Up Field Trip Parameters   *
and Cutoff Dates

Surprise field trips create conflicts between teachers, grade levels, and special area staff. The teacher who has spent a great deal of time to set up a special lesson should not discover suddenly that his class is on a field trip. A schedule should be published, and reminders should appear on the weekly memo to staff several weeks prior to the event. Cutoff dates have become necessary because of standardized tests. All teachers have a right to be concerned if there are too many field trips during the last few weeks of school. For schools that end in June, we recommend that there be no field trips after the middle of May. In other words, the principal should decide the closing date for class excursions in order to provide maximum class time for the last six weeks of school. If this is not done, a party atmosphere may replace the school's academic tone.

Personal Commentary/Notes: _____

_____

Establish Fire Drill Schedule   *
for the Year

Many states require a specific number of fire drills per year. Some also add to these demands the requirement that two thirds of the drills be held prior to the winter recess. This process makes sense because the procedures should be clear to staff and students alike. The latter part of this schedule should be flexible, because sometimes a break in the winter weather allows the administrator to hold a surprise fire drill or to make up for one that was canceled because of inclement weather.

Personal Commentary/Notes: _____

_____

August's Communications

* *Meeting With Parent-Teacher Organizations*

Principals should meet with the PTO or PTA president and with the entire executive board. Meeting dates were probably established in June to ensure they would not conflict with other school activities. The time, dates, and the purpose should now be reviewed and finalized. The topic of each meeting should be discussed, and new items that have a degree of urgency could be substituted for less important agenda ideas.

We recommend a hands-on approach for the principal when planning PTA activities. The principal should be an active participant in each meeting. A poor meeting or disgruntled parents ultimately become the principal's problem. Active participation will usually maximize the school's positive image and avoid the escalation of controversial issues. Your participation and expertise will guarantee a feeling of mutual support and a properly focused agenda. Many PTA programs can support the school's curriculum and address teacher and parent concerns. One additional thought submitted by a New York City principal is in the area of fundraising. This administrator has a list of items not funded by the board of education. His building has received a playground, benches for an outdoor reading area, and a new enclosed bulletin board as gifts from the PTA.

Another colleague has asked her PTA to sponsor after-school minicourses, purchase the Great Books program for accelerated children to use, and adopt PARP (Parents As Reading Partners). The building's PTA can enhance the academic program and improve the school's appearance and facilities.

*Personal Commentary/Notes:*_____

_____

* *Inspirational Speech*

At times, experienced principals don't make the most of this opportunity. Your entire staff deserves to hear your thoughts for the new year and your appreciation for their past efforts. While they are refreshed and rejuvenated from their summer vacations, we recommend you seize the moment. If the speech is successful, your faculty will look forward to the challenge ahead and be proud to be a member of the staff. This is your August meeting assignment—Due Date: First Day With Staff. Don't wing it!

*Personal Commentary/Notes:*_____

_____

Submit June Examination Grades   ✳
and Analysis to the Superintendent

Before school closes for the summer vacation, the principal must meet with each classroom teacher individually to discuss the results of student progress, standardized tests, and state assessments. The latter have become more prevalent throughout the nation in this era of accountability. Reviewing the results of testing affords us the opportunity to monitor the instructional program. Doing an item analysis might inform us of the fact that we are not teaching a particular topic properly or that it may not even be in our curriculum. At the present time, testing and comparing results with other districts is a reality principals must acknowledge. Understanding testing and being able to articulate the results is an additional skill that should be developed if it is not already a part of your expertise.

The superintendent will be very interested in the testing results. He or she will also be accountable and thus must be prepared to explain the data to the board of education and to the entire school community.

Personal Commentary/Notes: _____

_____

Principal's Newsletter   ✳

We believe that the principal's newsletter serves many valid educational purposes. It is a public relations document for the school year. It serves to increase the morale of both students and staff. It is an opportunity to give accolades for outstanding performance or service to the community. It informs the entire community about the school's progress and the extraordinary efforts of the students and teaching staff. The newsletter should also give the principal a sense of progress and perhaps assist in setting greater expectations for the year. The document should be forwarded to the superintendent, whom we hope will share your school's achievements with the board of education.

Personal Commentary/Notes: _____

_____

August's Planning

Summer Key   ✳
Staff Workshop

Everything we have discussed is a potential agenda item. Most principals give their key staff members an opportunity to submit items for the meeting.

Putting them in priority order maximizes the outcome. This is a time to focus on schoolwide concerns and strategies to improve the effectiveness of the entire school and to set specific future priorities.

*Personal Commentary/Notes:*_____

_____

✳ *Establish Goals and Projects*

These determinations should be the result of all your meetings with supervisors, teachers, parents, and students. Their implementation will demonstrate the collective vision of your school community.

It also indicates that we believe in the improvement process and resist resting on past laurels. The same expectation that we have for every staff member should be one of our own priorities. These goals may be short-term or multiyear expectations. A good example of a short-term goal might be to measure the number of cuts or discipline cards from last year to the conclusion of the present year in order to determine if our disciplinary plan is paying dividends. Some of the principal's projects that follow incorporate short- and long-term goals.

Specifying projects and listing them in priority order should provide attainable objectives to enhance your building's tone, curriculum, and facility. A principal from Texas formulated the following projects recently and reported that each was completed in a single school year:

1. Revise the Health curriculum and secure its approval from the superintendent and board of education.

2. Rewrite the portion of the disciplinary code dealing with misbehavior on the playground, cafeteria, and school buses to reduce problems perceived by staff.

3. Institute a new site-based management team to address the community's request to provide better building security.

4. Establish a student-faculty committee to ensure consistency in the selection of students to serve as class officers.

5. Complete the following facility improvement endeavors:
   a. Construct bookshelves in all third-grade classrooms.
   b. Construct bulletin boards for the Physical Education Department.
   c. Add electrical outlets in Rooms 12, 14, and 25.
   d. Construct a small basement area to house seasonal displays and play scenery.
   e. Construct shelves in the library and stock them with the required texts from each grade level.
   f. Remove graffiti and paint from both portable classrooms and all outside storage sheds.

g. Reline all parking spots and fill in all potholes prior to the spring recess.

Personal Commentary/Notes: _____

_____

School Opening Packet for Staff *

We are certain that in your files, your secretary or assistant principal, if you have one, will be able to obtain last year's school opening informational packet. Ideally, other ideas were added during the first month or two of the previous school opening period. Perform a yearly update to improve upon your file copy. Some topics may be duplicated in the teacher handbook. Here is a list you might want to consider when you develop your own:

1. Discuss first day of school bell schedule.

2. Outline first day of classes:
   a. Distribute emergency home contact cards.
   b. Review attendance procedures.
   c. Review how to handle injuries and the school nurse's office.
   d. Discuss special subjects schedules.
   e. Discuss curriculum.
   f. Discuss discipline.
   g. Discuss homework procedures.
   h. Distribute books (cover them for homework).
   i. Discuss class regulations and establish student expectations.
   j. Discuss location of important rooms such as the principal's office, the nurse's office, and so forth.

3. Give duty assignment job descriptions.

4. Hold first fire drill (preannounced).

5. Check for fire drill signs and know evacuation routes.

6. Review curriculum by grade level.

7. Review report card grading system.

Personal Commentary/Notes: _____

_____

Last-Minute Double-Checks *

One of the greatest gifts a principal can give to the staff is to guarantee a smooth opening. We make similar demands on teachers and request that they be prepared and organized from Day 1 of the school year. The final check of the items listed below is part of a principal's lesson plan or school opening plans. If these things are properly checked out, the school should open with an orderly tone.

1. Is the public address (PA) system working? Is the bell system working?

2. Are all fire extinguishers operable?

3. Are all emergency systems in order (exit lights, fire boxes, emergency exit directions in each room)?

4. Is there a flag in each classroom?

5. Are televisions in working order?

6. Do teachers have class lists?

7. Do teachers have texts and opening day supplies?

8. Are teachers aware of special health needs of children?

*Personal Commentary/Notes:*_____

_____

* Conduct Final Walk-Through With the Head Custodian

The principal provides the extra set of eyes in assessing the work of the custodial staff. The building may be clean, but the principal's responsibility is to find items that may affect a calm school opening or things that may prove to be a safety hazard. In one of our walk-throughs to test this item we found:

1. Fire exits not posted

2. No garbage cans in the cafeteria

3. Stairwell lights not operating

4. Three classrooms missing desks

5. The PA system not operating in the resource room

6. The classroom keys missing for three classroom teachers

7. Flags needed for several classrooms

8. The hallway floor by the gym's entrance doors somewhat slippery

These items can be viewed as minor problems, but by addressing them prior to the opening of school, the administrator has done his or her part to guarantee an orderly first day of classes.

*Personal Commentary/Notes:*_____

_____

August's Personnel

Complete Master Schedule　✻

A large magnetic board displayed in the outer main office and the principal's office depicts the Master Schedule and provides a quick reference. The schedule lists time, teacher's name, grade level, and subject (e.g., "Red 9:00 2S" means "Second grade Ms. Smith goes to physical education at 9:00 a.m."). Colored magnetic squares make conflicts easy to spot, and making changes becomes an easier task. Once the school year is under way, the posted Master Schedule can be converted to a weekly schedule.

In August, we double-check all building and grade-level assignments. If special teachers do not have their own rooms, we try to locate them in places that minimize their travel time. This is also the final check on staffing. If not completed, we must move to a crisis interviewing mode. Have some of your reliable substitutes on call and invite them to your first faculty meeting if they have to substitute during the first week.

Personal Commentary/Notes: _____

_____

Set Up Shared-Decision-Making　✻
Committee Meeting Dates

Many states now require shared-decision-making committees. Some are mandated by state law, and others have been negotiated by teacher unions. We endorse this form of collective decision making. The confident principal is not threatened by the input of the teaching staff. Some states now include parents and students on these teams. Every contemporary text on supervision extols the virtues of shared decision making. Setting the specific dates for these meetings in an elementary school is critical because teachers also attend faculty, grade-level, and districtwide committee meetings.

Personal Commentary/Notes: _____

_____

Suggested Correspondence　✻

Keeping parents informed of upcoming events and of suggestions for improving their child's success in school is greatly appreciated by parents. Tips on ways to handle problems facing elementary students can augment the school's efforts and give parents strategies that dovetail with the school's behavioral policies. Principals who share these kinds of insights display a sincere desire to work in tandem with the community in general and with parents in particular.

In addition to the letters sent to parents of all students, teachers, and support staff, many principals write to local police, fire departments, and local newspapers. One principal writes to all the local private and parochial schools, because "they are all our community's children." (See Resource C—Summer Letters to Parents.)

August's Checklists

August's Key Tasks and Reminders

Major Assignments	Date Started	Date Completed	Days on Task
Prepare school opening remarks for staff (be inspirational)			
Meet with all supervisors and teachers-in-charge			
Give presentation at board meeting, if required			
Set up field trip parameters and cutoff dates			
Establish fire drill schedule for year			
Complete master schedule			
Establish goals and projects			
Meet with Parent-Teacher Organization leaders			
Prepare opening-of-school packet for faculty			
Submit analysis of June examination and grade results to superintendent			
Complete last-minute double-checks			
Conduct final walk-through with head custodian			
Develop submission and publication schedule for principal's newsletter			

August's Communications Checklist

✔	Assignment
	Meet with Parent-Teacher Organization
	Send out opening-of-school letter to faculty and staff
	Submit June examination grades to superintendent
	Prepare principal's newsletter
	Send out letters to aides and monitors
	Mail out student teacher names and room assignments
	Send out opening-of-school letter and transportation information to parents and their kindergarteners

August's Planning Checklist

✔	Assignment
	Conduct Key Staff workshop
	Establish goals and projects
	Prepare opening day packet for staff
	Complete last-minute double-checks
	Conduct final walk-through with head custodian
	Plan new teacher orientation program

August's Personnel Checklist

✔	Finalize
	Complete master schedule
	Set up shared-decision-making committee meeting dates
	Send letters to parents, teachers, and support staff
	Fill remaining faculty and staff positions
	Review and update the substitute teacher list
	Revise staff directory

AUGUST CALENDAR

MONTH: AUGUST

YEAR: _____

MONDAY __	TUESDAY	WEDNESDAY __	THURSDAY	FRIDAY __	SATURDAY / SUNDAY __
MONDAY __	TUESDAY	WEDNESDAY __	THURSDAY	FRIDAY __	SATURDAY / SUNDAY __
MONDAY __	TUESDAY	WEDNESDAY __	THURSDAY	FRIDAY __	SATURDAY / SUNDAY __
MONDAY __	TUESDAY	WEDNESDAY __	THURSDAY	FRIDAY __	SATURDAY / SUNDAY __
MONDAY __	TUESDAY	WEDNESDAY __	THURSDAY	FRIDAY __	SATURDAY / SUNDAY __

Notes: _____

Chapter
Three

Have You Made Your Teachers Aware of How Important They Are to Children?

I have come to a frightening conclusion. I am the decisive element in the classroom. It is my daily mood that makes the weather. As a teacher, I possess tremendous power to make a child's life miserable or joyous. I can be a tool of torture or an instrument of inspiration. I can humiliate or humor; hurt or heal. In all situations, it is my response that decides whether a crisis will be escalated or de-escalated and a child humanized or dehumanized.

—Haim Ginott, *Teacher and Child*

Anyone who is not stimulated by the first few days of school should think about retirement. The children's faces and their obvious anticipation of meeting their new teachers creates an air of electricity. Teachers are excited and motivated. They want to get off on the right foot and set an excellent classroom tone.

The principal, having completed the summer tasks, is able to observe the fruits of his or her July and August labor. A smooth opening should be a source of pride. Perhaps only you, the principal, will be aware of how your intensive attention to detail made the start of the year successful. The accolades, however, will be given completely to your staff when you write your memo at the end of the first week of school. They do indeed deserve your compliments, but the authors of this text are aware that you were a competent silent partner.

Your physical presence throughout the building during those first few days will reassure the primary students and will also reacquaint you with your children in the intermediate grades. It's incredible how a good principal can maintain a caring image while enforcing school rules and regulations. Management-by-walking-around (MBWA) assures all administrators of a firsthand view of how the school is operating. All areas for improvement should be noted in your calendar to be addressed at a meeting or as a "tickler file" item for yourself for the following summer.

As you review your other September tasks, they should serve to remind you of how all-encompassing are the duties of an elementary principal. In secondary schools there are a host of chairpersons and assistant principals to whom tasks may be delegated. In most of our elementary schools, the "buck stops" at the principal's desk.

September's list of tasks is long and possibly intimidating. Not only are they numerous, but many are also open ended. As you can observe, each item often necessitates a host of subtopics. Although most of us don't have the luxury of assistant principals, it might be well to think of delegating certain tasks to experienced teachers, grade-level leaders, or specialists. Ultimately, you and your staff must set the standards for teacher aides, custodians, and parents. The throttle, like the school year, is open and running in overdrive. Your planning will calm the operational tone and help build in success.

Figure 3.1 is a Connecticut principal's September reminder to herself. In the highlights for the month, we will discuss many of these topics in greater detail.

FIGURE 3.1. Principal's September Reminder

_____ Mail welcome-back letters to (a) members of teaching staff and (b) teacher aides.

_____ Mail letters to parents regarding (a) parallel block scheduling and (b) inclusion services.

_____ Prepare materials for Faculty Orientation Day.

SAMPLE

1. Introduction of new staff members

2. Review of teacher handbook with emphasis on additions:

   a. Bomb threat procedures

   b. Fire drill routine in case one occurs during the lunch period

   c. Schedule for developing mutually agreed-upon Annual Professional Plans

   d. **S.T.A.R.S.** concept—our school's ethical code to which all are committed (**S**how respect to yourself and others; **T**ry your best; **A**ccept others; be **R**esponsible; **S**hare)

   Monthly assemblies will be conducted by our school's volunteer team to underscore these concepts.

3. Summer curriculum-writing projects

FIGURE 3.1. Continued

Each teacher participant will present an overview of the work accomplished.

4. Bus drill schedule

5. Learning specialist to discuss additional materials to be used in conjunction with our districtwide reading program

6. Requests for volunteers to teach in the
   a. After-School Reading Intervention program (Grades 1-5)
   b. After-School Homework Help program (Grades 3-5)

7. Discussion of this year's district goals
   – Prepare parent flyer regarding "Meet Your Teacher Night"
   – Meet with teachers (faculty meeting or staff development time) to discuss particulars of "Meet Your Teacher Night." Note: There will be four 20-minute sessions in order for parents with more than one child to be able to attend each teacher's presentation.

      1. Perhaps an outline on the chalkboard of pertinent points to be discussed will provide for good time management.

      2. Please provide parent-teacher conference sign-up sheets in your room in order to elicit the most convenient time to meet during the scheduled parent-teacher conference days or evenings. Confirmation forms may be obtained in the main office once the final determination has been made.

      3. A packet of information has been provided for distribution to each parent. It contains: Parent Handbook, Form for Emergency telephone numbers, Emergency Go-Home Drill letter, and so forth. Should a parent not attend the meeting, please be sure that the packet is sent home with the student.

      4. Suggestion: Children might like to write a note to parents and leave it on the desk for an answer.

      5. PTA suggests that an invitation to join PTA be extended on the chalkboard. They would also ask that you mention that they will host only four class parties per year (Halloween, Winter, Spring, End of Year). Adherence will eliminate unnecessary competition.

      6. Remember—a visually attractive room creates excellent public relations. This is especially true when children's work is displayed.

      THANK YOU FOR YOUR COOPERATION—it is greatly appreciated!

Prepare for the first PTA meeting. Be sure to include:
   a. District goals
   b. School goals
   c. Any new programs (Conflict Management; schoolwide ethical standards called S.T.A.R.S., etc.)
   d. Renovations to the building
   e. Student Council–planned activities (Volunteers' Tea, visits to local nursing homes, Thanksgiving collections, etc.)

September's Key Tasks

SEPTEMBER

* First Faculty Meeting and Orientation

The first faculty meeting sets the tone for the year. Combine the required opening of school information with an activity that focuses on the mission of the school. Introduce new staff, review state-mandated topics, highlight the faculty handbook, and review safety procedures. Make time to share an inspirational story. (See Resource A—Teacher Handbook.)

*Personal Commentary/Notes:*_____

_____

* Opening Preparation

Have bus drivers do a "dry run" the day before school opens to avoid late bus arrivals. Bring in cafeteria aides prior to the start of school to increase the efficiency of the first day's lunch periods. Cycle the bells for a day and check to see that they are all functioning properly. Check the public address system to make sure all rooms are receiving the announcements.

*Personal Commentary/Notes:*_____

_____

* First Parent-Teacher Night ("Meet Your Teacher Night")

"Meet Your Teacher Night" is a must for September or early October. It is our way to communicate to parents our building rules, grade-level course content, and teacher expectations. During the following month, after the first report cards are sent home, we recommend hosting a second night/day conference to enable teachers to discuss with each parent or guardian the progress of each child. Refer to the month of November for details. (See Resource D—Meet Your Teacher Night—Suggestions for Teachers.)

*Personal Commentary/Notes:*_____

_____

* Meeting With Security and Supervisory Staff

Meet with the security staff or teachers who assist in this regard to review procedures and to discuss their roles and responsibilities. Use role-playing techniques to remind staff of how to handle sensitive and difficult situations. Provide faculty supervisors of detention, cafeteria, and corridors with clear expectations and enforcement procedures. This will help minimize problems and confrontations.

Personal Commentary/Notes: _____

_____

New Students *

Be sure to personally meet students who are new to the school. Build this into the orientation program that the aide or secretary uses as part of the registration process. Follow up by monitoring the student's transition after the first few days of school. One principal invites new students to help in the office in July or August to familiarize them with the school.

Personal Commentary/Notes: _____

_____

New Teachers *

Meet with the new teachers to assist them in learning about the culture and practices of the school. Limit the specifics to only those topics that are necessary for a successful start to the year. Plan a series of follow-up sessions to cover issues that come up later in the year. Use the follow-up sessions as an opportunity to gain feedback about the school and to elicit ideas to improve and solve problems.

Personal Commentary/Notes: _____

_____

Reports *

Be sure to complete all required reports for the superintendent. Have your secretary keep a list of due dates and double-check important data to ensure accuracy. Daily attendance should be forwarded to the central office. Double-check class sizes to conform to school policy or teacher contract provisions.

Personal Commentary/Notes: _____

_____

Public Address System *

Meet with all staff who regularly use the public address system to review expectations, limits, appropriateness of announcements, and so forth. Limit the use of the system as much as possible to minimize class disruptions and to increase the impact of the few announcements that are authorized. If students help with the opening exercise, they must be adequately trained.

*Personal Commentary/Notes:*_____

_____

✴ *Cocurricular Advisers*

The cocurricular program of activities and clubs is a very important part of any school. All too often, major controversies develop over conflicts of days and times. To minimize these problems, meet with all of the advisers to review procedures, philosophy, financial rules, and scheduled dates. Develop and distribute a Student Activities Guidebook to help standardize procedures and responsibilities.

*Personal Commentary/Notes:*_____

_____

✴ *Safety Drills*

No area is more important than the safety of all students and staff. Be sure to follow all state and local regulations. Preannounce the first fire drill to make sure it serves as a model for all future drills. Check all safety equipment. Consult annually with the local police, fire, and ambulance officials.

*Personal Commentary/Notes:*_____

_____

✴ *Student Spirit*

Use the first few weeks of school to build school spirit. The first assembly should be well publicized and supported. Make sure that all bulletin boards are decorated and that the hallways are bright and cheerful. In an effective assembly, upper-grade students should be involved as you describe student council, special events, and after-school programs in order to motivate younger children.

*Personal Commentary/Notes:*_____

_____

✴ *Grant Proposals*

Work with the appropriate central office and building staff to identify and complete all required grant proposals and take advantage of some of the many optional grants that are available. Grant funds can serve as a significant supplement to the budget and provide money for opportunities for special programs and activities that would otherwise not be affordable. RIF (Reading Is Fundamental) is an example of an excellent program, now a fixture in most schools, which began with grant funds.

*Personal Commentary/Notes:*_____

_____

Staff Development ✻

Have each department or grade level develop a staff improvement plan for the year. This plan should be linked to building and district goals and priorities for the year. These plans will provide a framework to distribute funds and resources for staff development and to identify staff to attend appropriate conferences and training programs. These may also be logical follow-up objectives from last year's final evaluations. Your minimal expectation must be for each staff member to reach for a higher level of professional practice.

Personal Commentary/Notes: _____

_____

September's Communications

Memo to Staff ✻

We recommend that every elementary school principal produce a weekly memorandum for the staff. The purpose is to inform everyone about the events of the week, future activities, and due dates. School faculties do not always communicate with specials or with other grade levels. It is easy for a teacher and principal to have limited personal contact during the school day. The weekly memo helps bridge that communication gap. Teachers should be encouraged to submit items, thus providing a two-way aspect to this valuable means of communication. (See Resource E—Weekly Memo to Staff.)

Personal Commentary/Notes: _____

_____

Class Visits ✻

The administrator should visit classes to review the student handbook and emphasize expectations for student behavior. One principal developed a quiz on the handbook and gave out a gift certificate to the school store for the student with the best score in each class. These visits also give the administrative team a chance to interact with many of the faculty during the hectic first few days. In some states, many items, such as the review of disciplinary procedures and procedures for accusations of child abuse, are now the legal responsibility of the principal to communicate.

Personal Commentary/Notes: _____

_____

Reports on School Opening ✻

As the most visible spokesperson for your school, both oral and written reports to the major constituencies you serve are important. Use the first PTA and board of education meetings of the school year to highlight the opening of the building. You may wish to focus on the many positive faculty accomplishments completed over the summer and the smooth manner in which instruction began. A description of the adjustment of the new kindergarten usually adds a poignant touch.

*Personal Commentary/Notes:*_____

_____

✳ *Open School Night*

A special letter to all parents inviting them to attend Open School Night is a must. The letter should include the agenda for the evening, expectations, and a reminder to parents that this early meeting will focus on the curricular program, not on individual students. Provide refreshments in the cafeteria and invite the PTA to enroll new members, distribute their newsletter, and provide all parents with copies of PTA meeting dates and programs.

*Personal Commentary/Notes:*_____

_____

✳ *Parent's Newsletter*

A monthly letter sent home from the principal is an opportunity to share student and staff progress and awards as well as to inform parents about the most pressing issues that the school faces. The letter might include a calendar page with a list of student activities. Your PTA should be encouraged to include flyers advertising their events. Figure 3.2 is an example of a parent newsletter issued for the month of March.

*Personal Commentary/Notes:*_____

_____

FIGURE 3.2. Monthly Memo to Parents

Dear Parents,

March promises to be a most exciting month for our fourth graders.

In Science, the children will be involved in a variety of activities using circuits and switches as they discover the principles of electricity.

In Social Studies, students will learn about life on Long Island in the 19th century as well as the growth of whaling, fishing, and farming.

In Math, fourth graders will study decimals and fractions and will apply the skills learned to real-life problem-solving situations.

In Language Arts Extension, they will conduct a study of Jean Fritz, a writer of historical fiction.

As a reminder, during the week of March 11th, children will be taking the California Achievement Test.

We hope this newsletter assists you in sharing with your child the learning that is taking place in his or her classroom.

Sincerely,
Your Elementary School Principal

Parent Guidebook ✳

Home-school communication is critical to our success. We so believe that this is vital that we have included a Parent Guidebook to Principal Ayres's elementary school. (See Resource F—Parents' Elementary School Guidebook.)

Personal Commentary/Notes: _____

_____

Special Education ✳

Both classified and "504" students are entitled to a variety of accommodations. Be sure to formally remind faculty of their responsibilities in this area and to provide them with a list of students in each category along with the accommodations they should be receiving. This memo should be clearly marked as confidential to protect student privacy. Special education teachers should meet with staff members to emphasize this vital information. (See Resource G—Best Practices in Quality Education for Students With Severe Disabilities.)

Personal Commentary/Notes: _____

_____

Health Warning Letters ✳

Work closely with your nurse to give parents ample written notice of any deficiencies in meeting state and local immunization requirements. This is often a problem with transfer students. An early letter and a follow-up call can help make for a smooth transition to a new school. By all means, strictly adhere to your own state laws. Students often cannot be admitted without certain inoculations or vaccinations.

Personal Commentary/Notes: _____

_____

Problem Students ✳

Meet regularly with the school's Child Study Team to monitor problem students. The issues discussed at these meetings will often give you a heads-up on trends and issues in the community. Be sure the team includes the nurse, social worker, the school psychologist, counselors (if any), special education teachers, and any other staff on an as-needed basis. As elementary principals, we really assist our secondary colleagues by openly addressing behavioral problems. We should not simply push them ahead without working with parents/guardians. Obviously, we should document our efforts.

Personal Commentary/Notes: _____

_____

September's Planning

✳ Assemblies

Student assemblies are a wonderful opportunity to build school spirit and to share important information with the student body. Planning is the key to effective assemblies. Be sure to provide a seating chart, clear directions to staff, and a set of behavioral expectations for students. We frown upon assembly programs where students sit on the floor. The principal should run the first assembly and make it a model for the year.

*Personal Commentary/Notes:*_____

_____

✳ Open School Night

Preparation is the foundation for a successful Open School Night. Invite fifth graders to serve as guides for parents, who often do not know their way around the school. Have back-up schedules and student room assignments available for those parents who forget to bring the one they received with the letter inviting them to attend. Hold a brief assembly to start the evening and be sure to introduce your key personnel. Make sure you are available throughout the evening to answer questions and handle any difficult issues that may arise.

*Personal Commentary/Notes:*_____

_____

✳ Calendar

Develop and distribute a calendar that lists all the meetings for the month. This will help in finding common time for the many ad hoc and emergency meetings that must be held during the course of a month. This will also help faculty and improve attendance at the monthly faculty meeting, curriculum councils, safety squads, committee on special education, and so forth.

*Personal Commentary/Notes:*_____

_____

✳ Grade-Level and Special Department Newsletters

Maintaining regular communication between the school and home is vitally important. Some type of monthly newsletter should go home through the principal's office. Publish a schedule for the year and expect staff to submit items for inclusion. Student and staff awards, reminders, parenting advice, and curriculum changes should all be regular parts of the newsletter. Make sure the PTA and other parent-run organizations have the schedule and are invited to include announcements and flyers.

Personal Commentary/Notes: _____

_____

Student Activity Calendar ✳

Most schools have a rich and varied number of student clubs and service organizations. Many groups look for opportunities to raise money through such activities as car washes and bake sales. Coordination of these activities is important to avoid overlap and injured feelings. Spreading out schoolwide programs such as assemblies and fundraising activities reduces disruptions to the academic program. A well-communicated and well-maintained calendar will prevent many such problems.

Personal Commentary/Notes: _____

_____

Faculty Inservice ✳

Each state requires a variety of annual training sessions for faculty. The topics usually include affirmative action, right-to-know, sexual harassment, child abuse, HIV, and others. Develop a schedule for the year and make sure all faculty members are aware of the dates and topics.

Personal Commentary/Notes: _____

_____

Staff Development ✳

Most districts provide a number of training days for staff during the year. The principal should see these as opportunities to address buildingwide needs and concerns. A staff survey to identify topics for these programs is helpful. Design the day so that staff who do not regularly have the chance to interact will do so; this will help break down the traditional departmental and grade-level barriers that develop in elementary schools. New York State has recently passed a law to require 175 hours of staff inservice over a five-year period. Imagine this scheduling nightmare!

Personal Commentary/Notes: _____

_____

* Field Trips

No one will debate the value of field trips if they focus on quality places and reinforce the grade level's curriculum. We have found that often the field trip merely serves as a day off from school. To ensure that these excursions are valuable, here are some suggestions:

1. Make a list with your staff of quality places to host elementary children.

2. Yearly trips to the same local places by all grade levels diminishes the value of the experience.

3. Have teachers submit several objectives before you approve the trip.

4. Give priority approval to those that are tied to valuable objectives and to the grade's curriculum.

5. Guard against teachers who abuse the educational value of field experiences by scheduling an excessive number of trips.

*Personal Commentary/Notes:*_____

_____

September's Personnel

* Start-of-School Materials

One way to avoid an opening faculty meeting that merely reviews all of the little details is to mail faculty their handbooks and special memos a week before school begins. Although not all faculty will read these in advance, many of your staff will appreciate this opportunity to concentrate on getting their rooms and materials ready, rather than sitting in a long and sometimes boring opening meeting. It also provides an opportunity for teachers who have read the material to raise questions and offer suggestions.

*Personal Commentary/Notes:*_____

_____

* Emergency Information

Be sure to have the school secretary update and distribute to staff the emergency phone chain at the start of school. The chain is a valuable tool to use in weather emergencies or when a personal or schoolwide crisis occurs. This should also be done for each class so that parent "chains" can be established. Whether it be a weather emergency, electrical failure, or building fire, the chain calling system should be typed and distributed promptly.

*Personal Commentary/Notes:*_____

_____

Teacher Observations ✳

Evaluation of the teaching staff is one of the most important responsibilities of the principal. Develop a plan to ensure that all district and state deadlines for teacher observations and evaluations are met. Meet with any other supervisor to review the format and process for evaluating teachers. All too often, administrators lose in teacher incompetence hearings because of a mistake made in the process. Careful planning will avoid this and focus attention on the real issue—the quality of teaching in the classroom.

If the elementary principal held meaningful final evaluations in June, the goals for the new school year should be predictable. Plan as intensely for your finest staff members as you do for your new or weaker teachers. The excellent teacher needs to be motivated and perhaps to be given greater responsibilities.

Personal Commentary/Notes: _____

_____

Sunshine Committee ✳

The principal is the symbolic leader of the school, which is ideally thought of as a large family. As in any family, key events should be acknowledged. The principal should work closely with the Sunshine Committee to deal with the good and the bad that members of the staff encounter in their personal lives. Keep a supply of sympathy, thank-you, congratulation, and birthday cards on hand.

Personal Commentary/Notes: _____

_____

Objectives ✳

Each member of the principal's administrative team should be expected to develop objectives or goals for the year. Many of us work alone, but we may have curriculum directors to assist us. The principal should provide direction for the creation of the objectives and should meet individually with each person to approve the objectives for the year. An end-of-the-year meeting to assess progress of these objectives and goals should be a regular part of the evaluation process.

Many of us do not receive the assistance we need from supervisors stationed in the secondary schools. Elementary principals must be assertive and demand equal time for their building and for K-5 curriculum needs.

Personal Commentary/Notes: _____

_____

* School Directory

Creating and distributing a school directory to parents and students is a service that your community will appreciate. The directory should include important school, district, and community telephone numbers as well as a list of students by grades with their addresses and phone numbers. Be sure to give families the opportunity to opt out of the directory for privacy reasons.

Personal Commentary/Notes: _____

_____

* Counselors

For those of us who are blessed with counselors and social workers, the week before school starts is often the most busy and hectic of the year. Providing an additional week for these staff members and bringing them in early will help ensure that the needs of your atypical children are met.

Personal Commentary/Notes: _____

_____

September's Checklists

September's Key Tasks and Reminders

Major Assignments	Date Started	Date Completed	Days on Task
Conduct first faculty meeting			
Conduct "dry runs" for opening of school			
Prepare and host "Meet Your Teacher Night"			
Meet with security staff and faculty supervisors			
Oversee orientation of new students			

Major Assignments	Date Started	Date Completed	Days on Task
Meet with new teachers			
Complete reports for superintendent			
Provide orientation for all who use the public address system			
Meet with all cocurricular advisers to review expectations and procedures			
Hold required safety drills			
Begin student spirit-building activities			
Complete annual grant proposals			
Collect department staff development plans			

September's Communications Checklist

✔	Assignment
	Compose weekly memo to the staff
	Make personal visits to classes to emphasize expectations for student behavior
	Report to the PTA, superintendent, and board of education on school opening
	Send Open School Night invitation to all parents
	Write article for parent newsletter
	Update and distribute Parents' Elementary School Guidebook
	Write and distribute memo to faculty on special education accommodations
	Send warning letters home to students who lack required immunizations
	Attend monthly Child Study Team and Pupil Personnel Service meetings to discuss problem students

September's Planning Checklist

✔	Assignment
	Develop assembly procedures and plans
	Prepare for Open School Night
	Develop calendar of monthly meetings
	Publish the monthly newsletter
	Maintain and review student activity calendar
	Schedule required inservice faculty meetings about affirmative action, right-to-know, child abuse, HIV, and so forth
	Plan for buildingwide staff development activities
	Monitor field trip requests

September's Personnel Checklist

✔	Finalize
	Mail faculty start-of-school materials
	Distribute emergency staff telephone chain
	Set up schedule of teacher observations and evaluations in coordination with assistant principals and department chairpersons
	Meet with faculty Sunshine Committee to plan activities for year
	Review written objectives with each member of the administrative team
	Secure residence data to develop school directory
	Budget an additional week for counselors before school opens

SEPTEMBER CALENDAR

MONTH: SEPTEMBER

YEAR: _____

MONDAY	TUESDAY	WEDNESDAY	THURSDAY	FRIDAY	SATURDAY / SUNDAY
___	___	___	___	___	___
___	___	___	___	___	___
___	___	___	___	___	___
___	___	___	___	___	___
___	___	___	___	___	___

Notes: _____

Chapter
Four

Do Teachers Feel a Part of Your Team?

Goose Sense

Next fall, when you see geese heading south for the winter, flying along in "V" formation, you might consider what science has discovered as to why they fly that way. As each bird flaps its wings, it creates an uplift for the bird immediately following. By flying in "V" formation, the whole flock adds at least 71 percent greater flying range than if each bird flew on its own.

People who share a common direction and sense of community can get where they are going more quickly and easily, because they are traveling on the thrust of one another. When a goose falls out of formation, it suddenly feels the drag and resistance of trying to go it alone and quickly gets back into formation to take advantage of the lifting power of the bird in front. If we have as much sense as a goose, we will stay in formation with those people who are headed the same way we are.

When the head goose gets tired, it rotates back in the wing and another goose flies point. It is sensible to take turns doing demanding jobs, whether with people or with geese flying south. Geese honk from behind to encourage those up front to keep up their speed. What messages do we give when we honk from behind?

Finally, and this is important, when a goose gets sick or is wounded by gunshot, and falls out of formation, two other geese fall out with that goose and follow it down to lend help and protection. They stay with the fallen goose until it is able to fly or until it dies; and only then do they launch out on their own or with another formation to catch up with their group. If we have the sense of a goose, we will stand by each other like that.

—Author Unknown

If the school opened smoothly in September, our passion for excellence and dedication to detail was amply rewarded. However, we strongly disagree with those who exhale and believe that October will be a lull until the increased tempo of the November and December holiday excitement. The pace you've set must be maintained and the planning accelerated to harness your high expectations for the entire first half of the school year.

By October, your faculty and students will ideally have settled into the established school routines. One look at the key tasks should be enough to focus on the challenges ahead. Three tasks usually dominate our thoughts. First, there is an Open School Night for parents. Our desire is to showcase our excellent staff, course offerings, and the physical plant while nurturing a positive relationship with students' parents.

This parent-teacher conference goes beyond the general discussions of grade-level requirements, homeroom expectations, and tours of the building. We should now be prepared to discuss each child's progress with parents or guardians. We recommend a faculty meeting to help staff members to fully understand the goals of the conference and, more important, to learn how to communicate with parents. Hint: Describe behavior, don't label children using psychological terms. For example, "Your child pushes other children" is a good description. "Your child shows an aggressive and hostile tendency" is asking for a confrontation with parents.

October offers the school an opportunity to make a holiday such as Halloween a positive rather than a destructive occasion. We do not advise having day-long costume parties and parades. Effective principals will have an after-school PTA-sponsored party. Awards for best costumes and wholesome games may be planned.

Many of us use the after-school party to elicit a pledge that children will not trick-or-treat after 7 p.m. This has helped eliminate many evening injuries, and parents have been pleased with this alternative celebration. Some of our middle school colleagues are now doing similar programs.

The next task is the start of a six-month-long budget process for the following year. This is an excellent example of long-range planning. Every part of your building and the school's academic program must be considered.

One elementary principal developed a system of budget subcommittees to explore the school's immediate and future needs. The classroom committee interviewed all teachers to ascertain their "wish lists" of items for their own classrooms, the library, or the office. Within a month, the principal had a list from everyone on the staff, in priority order, that included furniture, painting needs, shelving, bulletin boards, and other classroom priorities. Grade-level committees also met to determine computer and textbook needs. Curriculum-writing projects were also suggested to align subject matter with new state mandates. Special area departments did the same. A building committee, including the head custodian, submitted plans to improve the aesthetics. Obviously, the principal met with the building custodians and the district superintendent of buildings and grounds to determine the high-cost capital projects. Items such as roofs, new boilers, windows, and major renovations need the expertise and support of district officials.

Elementary school staffing is usually addressed early in the second half of the school year. Emergency hirings do occur when there are sudden illnesses, child care leaves, and special education enrollment increases and if there are obligations to add a class when there are contractual agreements on maximum class size.

We have found that when principals make their presentations later in the year, the thoroughness of the planning they do in October is the key to whether their budget requests are accepted by the superintendent and the board of education.

All of the authors agree that by the end of October, every new teacher should have been observed at least once.

October's Key Tasks

* **Open School Night**

Careful planning for Open School Night is critical to the success of the evening. Be sure that the school looks good, that extra student schedules are available, and that plenty of coffee and refreshments are provided in the cafeteria. Use one of your student service groups to provide guides to help parents find their way to each child's classes.

Ideally, it would be appropriate to have a parent night in September to discuss grade-level requirements, homework expectations, and the means to improve parent-teacher communication. The second meeting, in October or November, should be to talk with parents or guardians about the progress and behavior of individual students. Some teacher contracts may limit the number of evening meetings. Half-day school conferences have been utilized, but in an era of working parents, these are at times problematic. Day and evening conferences are obviously the ideal system to reach out to parents.

Principals should not take for granted that every teacher is capable of conducting a professional conference with parents. We recommend a discussion at a faculty meeting, role-playing exercises, and a memorandum to staff to provide some advice and guidelines.

*Personal Commentary/Notes:*_____
_____

Screening New Entrants ✳

Although this is an ongoing process throughout the year, late admissions to your school should be properly screened. We offer the following recommendations:

1. Evidence of state health requirements must be presented (inoculations and vaccinations).

2. Residency documents must be presented to qualify students to be educated in your school district or your particular school.

3. Have secretary trained to perform steps 1 and 2 prior to the student's meeting with you or your academic screening committee.

4. Assess students and provide a process for this information to be given to the classroom teacher.

5. Immediately take action if a new student is in need of special services.

Personal Commentary/Notes: _____

_____

Review All Students in Need ✳
of Special Services

This is a guarantee that no student "slips through the cracks" in your school and that you are aware of the trends in your student body. You should know the number of children receiving services in categories such as Chapter I, English as a second language, resource room, speech, and special education. As the principal, you should be aware of the IEP (Individual Educational Plan) and the focus of your staff's instructional objectives for each child. On the surface, this sounds like an awesome responsibility, but many principals have an annotated file for each child receiving such services. When meeting with a parent, the principal can briefly glance at the child's file, giving parents a sense of confidence in the school, principal, and classroom teachers.

We also advise that letters written to parents should be in English and in the language of newly arrived immigrants. This accommodation is a second and often more meaningful welcome letter.

Personal Commentary/Notes: _____

_____

Review Plan for Faculty Meetings ✳

We believe that faculty meetings are often lost opportunities for relevant in-service training. Utilize a committee to host meetings that truly support your instructional or disciplinary goals.

Personal Commentary/Notes: _____

_____

✳ *Hold First Site-Based Committee Meeting*

A typical agenda should include the following:

1. Review last year's work, accomplishments, and disappointments.
2. Select a new facilitator and review his or her duties.
3. Set the goals for the year. Sometimes it's helpful to select ideas from the entire staff.
4. Be sure to keep a timetable for the meetings, because both staff and parents have other responsibilities.

*Personal Commentary/Notes:*_____

_____

✳ *Budget Development*

Developing the budget is a long and detailed process. Give your staff as much lead time as possible. Provide a clear timeline of meetings, review sessions, adjustments, and so forth. Set conceptual parameters and ask that new programs and additional staffing needs be handled separately from the routine budgetary needs. Most elementary principals meet with all grade levels and with all of their specialized teachers. Curriculum needs, textbooks, furniture, and individual room improvements are open for discussion. We also include the custodians to help complete our plant improvement requests. As you will note, the budget process is a monthly ongoing task.

*Personal Commentary/Notes:*_____

_____

✳ *Testing Program*

Work with the staff running your standardized testing program to develop a comprehensive schedule for the year. Often there are both district and state requirements. Put yourself in the shoes of the students taking the tests to be sure that they have been placed on the calendar at times that do not conflict with other major school events and activities. Plan for the sharing of results with students, parents, and staff. Elementary principals must be more sensitive than their secondary colleagues because of our students and their parents' anxiety. A note sent home giving calming advice to parents should help everyone to relax. Teachers should attempt to depressurize the testing process. It's appropriate to prepare students for the test's format, but overemphasizing the importance of the examination is usually counterproductive. If principals put great pressure on their staff during testing days, you can be sure this anxiety will be transmitted to students.

*Personal Commentary/Notes:*_____

_____

Halloween ✳

Work with your PTA and student government officers to plan a positive activity for Halloween weekend. Just to be safe, however, add overnight security to monitor the building. Taking extra precautions will save you a lot of headaches. Educators are trying to change a holiday associated with too much violence and vandalism into a more wholesome celebration. This should be the principal's objective as well.

Personal Commentary/Notes: _____

_____

Intermediate Grades ✳

Meet with the leaders of your highest grade level (fifth or sixth grade) to plan and review the major events for the year. These should include fundraising activities, class trips, class photographs, moving-up exercises, concerts, and the school yearbook. Plan to hold a meeting of the entire class to set the tone for the year and to clearly establish behavioral expectations for the many special events of the year.

Your oldest students should be of great use: assisting on the playground, helping with reading in kindergarten classes, serving as monitors, and leading the safety squad. (We prefer that this meeting take place in September if possible.) Peer-mediation training has enabled the oldest children to gain status from doing good deeds rather than from bullying younger children. The oldest children should be a valuable school resource.

Personal Commentary/Notes: _____

_____

Homecoming ✳

A successful homecoming weekend provides a real boost to school spirit. This is not an exclusively high school activity. We recommend the involvement of every school, all clubs, and community organizations in general. As soon as the theme is determined, solicit staff, students, and parents to plan for a float and participants who will march in the parade. Monitor all plans for the homecoming with safety, good sportsmanship, and clean fun in mind. Send a special letter home to share plans and to remind all of our safety expectations. This is a good way to prevent problems from occurring.

Personal Commentary/Notes: _____

_____

* *President's Education Award*

Alert all grade teachers about this national award contest. Winners' awards are presented at an end-of-the-year assembly program and at local board of education meetings. This can be an integral part of your public relations initiative.

*Personal Commentary/Notes:*_____

_____

* *Board of Education Recognition*

Elementary schools are too often left out of plans for the traditional board of education recognition days. Be sure to plan events that showcase your students' many talents, interests, and service to the community. Invite board members to visit classes and to participate at PTA events and at any other activities that highlight the elementary school program. Too often, high school teams and student achievement dominate board meetings. We believe elementary principals should meet and prepare to showcase their schools and children. Remember, you and your parents deliver the most "yes" votes in every school budget. This, too, is a monthly reminder for elementary principals.

*Personal Commentary/Notes:*_____

_____

* *Emergency Drills*

A principal must attend to the required fire and emergency drills. Be proactive and invite the local fire and emergency officials to attend one of your drills to give you feedback and suggestions. Make the first drill the best drill, for it sets the tone for the rest of the year.

Local fire and police officials are very generous with their time. They often meet with classes and grade levels to discuss fire safety and security. They make the drills important to our students and convey many safety tips for school and home as well.

*Personal Commentary/Notes:*_____

_____

October's Communications

* *Board of Education Presentation*

Identify programs that the board and community should learn about. Work with the appropriate staff to prepare and deliver a presentation at each board of education meeting. Not only will the board be more supportive, but typically the local press will provide positive coverage in the paper. They love to have pictures of young students engaged in school activities. Spelling contest winners, children who have performed good deeds, and art award winners should receive recognition at board meetings. This item is in addition to inviting board members to personally attend your school's activities.

Personal Commentary/Notes: _____

_____

PTA Meetings *

The principal should meet regularly with the PTA leadership to help plan their monthly meetings. Suggesting staff to speak, coordinating fundraising efforts, and other activities are all part of a successful PTA. As principal, you should report at each meeting on the major events and issues that parents are interested in and concerned about. This is a great time to put to rest those rumors that always develop.

Elementary PTAs are the largest and most active in the school system. They are enthusiastic and an excellent audience for school-based programs. PTA meetings in which teachers participate are well attended. Outside experts on topics such as school safety, testing, Megan's law, homework, and curriculum are usually very successful.

The PTA can be an incredible support system for the school. Principals should nurture their relationships with parents by listening to their concerns and suggestions. Having parents on shared-decision-making teams assures the school of their participation and input. The PTA meeting is a vital part of the school's public relations program.

Personal Commentary/Notes: _____

_____

K-12 Principals' Meetings *

A monthly meeting with the middle and high school principals greatly improves curriculum articulation and the transition to the middle school. We believe it is destructive and counterproductive for any principal to denigrate another school's work. It is evident that elementary leaders can learn from their 6-8 and 9-12 colleagues, and the opposite is true as well.

Many of your staff members are part of districtwide departments such as art, physical education, special education, English as a second language, and nurses. Meeting with the leaders of these K-12 departments helps all principals to keep current on district and state changes.

Personal Commentary/Notes: _____

_____

✳ *Local Service Clubs*

As principal, you have a responsibility to be the chief public spokesperson for the school. Joining your area service clubs, sharing school news, and providing students to help with activities often pays dividends in the form of donations of money and equipment as well as support for the budget and school in general. We have found that organizations such as Kiwanis, Rotary, Elks, and Lions provide speakers for career days, help to involve children in community service projects, and offer a great opportunity to improve the school's public relations initiative.

*Personal Commentary/Notes:*_____

_____

✳ *Bulletin Boards*

Develop a schedule for the use of bulletin boards and showcases around the building. Grade levels, departments, student clubs, and organizations should be given responsibility for many of the displays. A building that looks good to the eye makes a positive first impression on visitors and parents.

As principals, we are blessed with teachers who take great pride in the appearance of their classrooms. The entire building is a principal's responsibility, and this can easily become a charge to a shared-decision-making committee. Many schools have students and parents paint large, attractive murals in hallways.

*Personal Commentary/Notes:*_____

_____

✳ *Thank-You Notes*

A principal can never send enough thank-you notes. Set up a system with your secretary to do this, and personalize as many notes as possible. We have found that at times we take our best teachers for granted. We become so involved with new staff and those experiencing difficulty that we may neglect our superstars. One suggestion from a Texas principal was to list the names of his finest staff members the week before the spring and winter recess and send them notes of appreciation twice a year. This is in addition to their outstanding evaluations.

*Personal Commentary/Notes:*_____

_____

✳ *School Profile*

Updating the school profile and the data fact sheet keeps community members, boards of education, the superintendent, and your own staff current with information about your school. Staff members should have copies, because they are often called on to be informal public relations ambassadors at community gatherings and events or while shopping at the local mall. Never take for granted the accomplishments of your school, teachers, and students. Even a third-place ranking in a local county or state contest adds to the image of your school. You can be sure the parents of the children mentioned will become part of your support system.

Personal Commentary/Notes: _____

_____

October's Planning

Capital Budget ✳

Develop a five-year capital improvement list of projects to address the essential building needs. This list should be updated annually with the district's director of capital projects. Though we stressed this in our introduction to this chapter, many of our K-5 colleagues do not see big-ticket items as their responsibility. The truth is that we often do not get the new gymnasium, roof, windows, and major renovations the first time they are requested. However, the annual reminder often gets the project budgeted in the following school year. No one else has your "eyes." The principal should have the entire plant in his or her line of sight.

As part of the budgetary process and the introduction of new technology, the library must be of prime consideration. Recent technological advances are revolutionizing this area and are adding new meaning to the phrase *library media center.* In the library, we now find such tools as:

✳   Computerized card catalogs and circulation systems

✳   CD-ROM-based reference tools, including electronic encyclopedias and magazine collections

✳   Electronic atlases, concordances, dictionaries, and almanacs

✳   Videodisc players with pictorial capabilities that can store entire collections of art galleries

✳   A wide range of word-processing programs that allow students to create high-quality reports

✳   Online access to commercial databases and the World Wide Web via the Internet

✳   A wide range of educational programs designed to permit practice, tutorials, and simulations

And the list gets bigger every day! Remember, your ability to implement these programs and to design a top-flight library media center depends on your ability to properly budget for the equipment and tools that can make it happen.

*Personal Commentary/Notes:*_____

_____

✳ *American Education Week*

This is a week to invite members of the community into your school to see the best you have to offer. Showcase your top academic students and provide each visitor with a package of materials to educate him or her about your strengths and needs as a school. Don't lose this opportunity to highlight your chorus, band, science projects, or art portfolios. Parents should go home feeling enthusiastic about your programs, teachers, and students.

*Personal Commentary/Notes:*_____

_____

✳ *Principals' Meetings*

Joining the local principals' or administrators' organization is a must. Attend at least one meeting a year. Networking will give you a local support base and friendly colleagues to use as a sounding board about problems you face. Some local colleges sponsor "collegial circles," where principals present model programs and offer the exchange of school visits. These local conferences are enhanced by the fact that schools in close proximity often have similar issues. Make certain you have the phone numbers of a few principals in other school districts. The elementary principalship is often a lonely job. You need this additional support system!

*Personal Commentary/Notes:*_____

_____

October's Personnel

✳ *Teacher Observations*

Read each and every teacher observation written by your chairperson, directors, and administrative staff. Not only will you have a good handle on your staff, but you will also be able to make this a part of the evaluation of each of your K-12 chairpersons and directors. We have an excellent teacher job description submitted by a New York school district that we utilize as an inservice for anyone who evaluates our teachers. It demonstrates the incredible number of skills an excellent teacher must possess. (See Resource H—Teacher Job Description.)

Personal Commentary/Notes: _____

_____

Staff Breakfast *

A principal needs to attend to the social side of the staff. Holding periodic, informal staff breakfasts is a way to bring the faculty together.

Personal Commentary/Notes: _____

_____

October's Checklists

October's Key Tasks and Reminders

Major Assignments	Date Started	Date Completed	Days on Task
Prepare for Open School Night			
Screen new entrants			
Review students in need of special services			
Review plans for faculty meetings			
Hold first site-based committee meeting			
Set budget development timelines and parameters			
Coordinate testing program for year			
Plan Halloween dance or alternative activities			
Meet with grade-level leaders			
Plan homecoming parade and activities			
Notify teachers of national award contests			
Coordinate board of education recognition day			
Conduct fire and emergency drills			

October's Communications Checklist

✔	Assignment
	Plan monthly board of education presentation
	Help plan monthly PTA meeting
	Schedule meetings with elementary and/or middle school principals
	Schedule attendance at meetings of local service clubs
	Review bulletin boards and school exhibits
	Send thank-you notes to groups who helped with Back-to-School Night
	Update school and student test data fact sheet and school profile

October's Planning Checklist

✔	Assignment
	Prepare a list of capital improvements for budget process
	Plan American Education Week activities
	Schedule area principals' meeting dates on calendar

October's Personnel Checklist

✔	Finalize
	Check on teacher observation process
	Hold breakfast for staff

OCTOBER CALENDAR

MONTH: OCTOBER

YEAR: _____

MONDAY ___	TUESDAY ___	WEDNESDAY ___	THURSDAY ___	FRIDAY ___	___ SATURDAY / SUNDAY ___
MONDAY ___	TUESDAY ___	WEDNESDAY ___	THURSDAY ___	FRIDAY ___	___ SATURDAY / SUNDAY ___
MONDAY ___	TUESDAY ___	WEDNESDAY ___	THURSDAY ___	FRIDAY ___	___ SATURDAY / SUNDAY ___
MONDAY ___	TUESDAY ___	WEDNESDAY ___	THURSDAY ___	FRIDAY ___	___ SATURDAY / SUNDAY ___
MONDAY ___	TUESDAY ___	WEDNESDAY ___	THURSDAY ___	FRIDAY ___	___ SATURDAY / SUNDAY ___

Notes: _____

Chapter Five

Does Your Staff Teach Values During the Holidays?

I want my students to learn that an individual can matter, can make a difference, can rebel against an unjust authority, can stand up against group pressure, can intercede on another's behalf.

I want to make them stronger and better people, to encourage them to be the social activist of their time, the ones who will take responsibility, who will be the Resisters and the Rescuers.

I want them to believe that the world is repairable and to encourage action in repairing whatever part of their world is torn by injustice or evil.
—Excerpts from presentation by Karen Shawn

In November, calm and routine should have replaced the hectic pace of the school's opening months. First report cards will be sent home, because most of us will have completed 10 weeks of school. In the Sunbelt states, this may occur a month earlier, because students return to school in August. Many school systems have kindergarten report cards distributed during one-on-one conferences with teachers. This makes sense if the school hosts day and evening meetings with parents to meet the needs of working couples and guardians. The board of education often allows a half-day of school at the elementary level for this purpose.

Although the academic environment is clearly the priority, November, which culminates with the Thanksgiving Day vacation, is also an important time for schoolwide service projects. Many school districts across the nation are adopting community service requirements, hoping to motivate all K-12 students to get involved. Learning to receive pleasure from helping others is a value we wish to encourage. Don't let anyone tell you that we don't teach values! Obviously, we should also not forget the historical significance of Thanksgiving as part of our social studies curriculum.

November is also a time when classroom visitations should be in full swing. This process should never be minimized. Through thorough supervision, the elementary principal is empowered to build an outstanding faculty. Teachers recommended for tenure should be outstanding. If you settle for less, your staff will never be outstanding! Never minimize the impact that this process has on your staffing. Ultimately, you are the person most responsible for the quality of your teachers.

Within a few months, you will have to make rehiring recommendations. Some contracts afford staff members several months' notice if they are to be dismissed. Reality dictates that as early as November, the principal may have only a couple more months to make the final decisions. It's critical to do your observations early and often, especially for nontenured teachers.

November's Key Tasks

Faculty Meeting *

Faculty meetings can easily become routine and boring to teachers. Make the faculty meeting a combination of "feel good" announcements about staff and intellectually stimulating presentations. Provide short readings as preparation for discussions on current topics and controversies. Bring community speakers in. Ask for feedback and involve the staff in planning the meeting.

Personal Commentary/Notes: _____

_____

Teacher Observations *

Make time in your schedule each week to conduct one or more formal observations and to informally visit a variety of classes. Be sure to follow up on each visit with a short note to the teacher. Let your faculty know up front your approach and philosophy concerning observations and visits. Recognizing the time when you shouldn't enter a classroom is as important as making a formal observation.

Most principals concentrate on new or nontenured teachers. Your regular staff should be observed as well. Your encouraging comments serve to motivate your "old pro staff." Having them mentor young colleagues or teach demonstration lessons serves the dual purpose of inservice for your teachers and a renewal of pride for your experienced staff members.

Personal Commentary/Notes: _____

_____

* Grades

Review the first marking period grades submitted by teachers and specials. Pay attention to situations with an unusually high number of students who are earning failing grades. Work with every new teacher to address and understand the circumstances producing their grades. We advise that the elementary principal review every new teacher's report cards before sending them home. This is a time-consuming process in a large building, but if the task can't be delegated to an assistant principal, do it yourself! It will be time well spent and will avoid a host of potential problems.

Personal Commentary/Notes: _____

_____

* School Play

The school play is a wonderful opportunity to showcase the talents of your students and staff. It can also be a flashpoint for controversy and problems. Advance work with the play adviser, a review of the script, and a preview by attending a rehearsal will give you the opportunity to address any problems before they become a public issue.

We also recommend that you review the music chosen for the forthcoming winter concert. Many principals have wonderful performances, only to be criticized for music that was too religious or the opposite. If the district has a K-12 director of music, principals should utilize his or her services.

Personal Commentary/Notes: _____

_____

* School Service Projects

More and more educators recognize the importance and value of participating in service projects. The entire community views such involvement as important in educating the "whole child." Coordinate such activities, and be sure to use the impact of student service to benefit the school as well as the community.

Obviously, November gives students the opportunity to have a food drive to help their less fortunate neighbors and perhaps the elderly or shut-ins.

Personal Commentary/Notes: _____

_____

November's Communications

PTA Presentation ✳

Use your monthly PTA presentation to share plans for upcoming events and to ask for parental help and input on important projects and issues. By involving parents on a regular basis, you will allow them to feel part of the school and will ensure their support at budget time.

With a national attack on education, these meetings offer us a means to a greater level of respect. Changing standards and the end of social promotion in many schools should make our PTA agenda enlightening and stimulating.

Personal Commentary/Notes: _____

_____

Holiday Issues ✳

One of the most sensitive and potentially explosive issues a principal faces is handling holiday parties, decorations, sales, and so forth. Be sure you are familiar with the district policies that govern each of these issues. Monitor all displays and concert programs to make sure policies are followed. A reminder memo to all staff each year outlining the key expectations will avoid problems later.

This concern should also be addressed at PTA meetings and in faculty handbooks. One principal sends home a letter to discuss special arrangements for Thanksgiving celebrations. Another principal recognizes that holidays are not always joyous times for everyone. She offers the services of the school's psychologist in letters such as the one outlined in the appendix dealing with children of divorced parents. (See Resource I—Helping Children Cope at Holiday Time.)

Personal Commentary/Notes: _____

_____

Board of Education Presentation ✳

Use the monthly board of education meeting to recognize students and staff for the awards they receive. The board will relish the opportunity to congratulate students and staff for their special accomplishments. A principal from New

Jersey keeps a "Good News Box" on his secretary's desk, and teachers drop in items to be shared with the board and the PTA.

*Personal Commentary/Notes:*_____

_____

✳ *Cultural Diversity*

Use the holiday spirit of the season to promote cultural diversity and the appreciation of a variety of religions. Make this a part of the instructional program to avoid any church-state separation issues. One school sponsors an annual Intercultural Unity Festival each year that features foods and dances of the cultures represented in the school and community population.

*Personal Commentary/Notes:*_____

_____

✳ *Student Service Awards*

Develop a type of Student-of-the-Month award program. Provide the local press with a picture and a brief article about the student. Such programs promote school spirit and put your school in a positive light with the community. A principal on Long Island eats lunch once a month on a Friday with his students of the month. This is an honor for K-5 children, and parents have been favorably impressed.

*Personal Commentary/Notes:*_____

_____

November's Planning

✳ *Enrollment Projections*

As part of the budgetary development process, an accurate enrollment projection is very important. Work with the pre-K program administrators and census takers to obtain up-to-date figures for the incoming kindergarten class, and monitor transfer numbers to make the appropriate adjustments. An accurate enrollment projection will give you credibility with the superintendent and the board. Remember that certain teacher contracts require classes to be split when they reach a specific number. These possibilities must be flagged for your superintendent or the assistant superintendent for personnel.

*Personal Commentary/Notes:*_____

_____

Holiday Events ✳

This is the time of year to schedule events that open the school up to the community. Reach out to parents, grandparents, and senior citizens by inviting them to special lunches, plays, and concerts. Many schools provide seniors with passes to all school events. Some schools designate the dress rehearsal for the play as a free show for all the senior citizens in the community so that they can attend during the day rather than coming out at night.

Personal Commentary/Notes: _____

_____

Conferences ✳

Attending professional conferences is an important way to network, to stay on top of key trends, and to "recharge" one's batteries. The elementary principal's national conferences, usually in February or March, offer a variety of workshops. A weeklong summer institute such as the IDEA Fellow program or the Harvard Principals' Institute can supply ideas and materials for years to come. We believe principals should share their own successful practices and programs with colleagues. Some local communities have principal meetings on a regular schedule. These are an excellent way to learn what is happening in other districts.

Personal Commentary/Notes: _____

_____

Inclement Weather ✳

Review procedures for inclement weather, late openings, school closings, and early dismissals. Be sure the snow chain is up-to-date and distributed well before the first snowflake falls. All communications should include radio and television stations that carry area school closings.

Personal Commentary/Notes: _____

_____

November's Personnel

Library Media Center ✳

The library media center should be the hub of any elementary school. Work with the librarian to plan a series of events and programs that encourage the use of the resources available in the library. These events might include author book talks, special displays, a book fair, summer reading lists, and so forth.

*Personal Commentary/Notes:*_____

_____

November's Checklists

November's Key Tasks and Reminders

Major Assignments	Date Started	Date Completed	Days on Task
Conduct monthly faculty meeting			
Do teacher observations			
Review grades by teacher and department			
Preview school play			
Encourage schoolwide service projects			

November's Communications Checklist

✔	Assignment
	Prepare PTA presentation
	Compose school policy memo on holiday party, decorations, sales, and so forth
	Prepare board of education presentation
	Foster appreciation of other religions and cultures
	Initiate student service awards program

November's Planning Checklist

✔	Assignment
	Complete enrollment projections
	Schedule holiday dance, art show, and community service events
	Apply for funds and permission to attend conferences
	Review procedures for inclement weather

November's Personnel Checklist

✔	Finalize
	Library media center

NOVEMBER CALENDAR

MONTH: NOVEMBER

YEAR: _____

MONDAY _____	TUESDAY _____	WEDNESDAY _____	THURSDAY _____	FRIDAY _____	_____ SATURDAY / SUNDAY _____
MONDAY _____	TUESDAY _____	WEDNESDAY _____	THURSDAY _____	FRIDAY _____	_____ SATURDAY / SUNDAY _____
MONDAY _____	TUESDAY _____	WEDNESDAY _____	THURSDAY _____	FRIDAY _____	_____ SATURDAY / SUNDAY _____
MONDAY _____	TUESDAY _____	WEDNESDAY _____	THURSDAY _____	FRIDAY _____	_____ SATURDAY / SUNDAY _____
MONDAY _____	TUESDAY _____	WEDNESDAY _____	THURSDAY _____	FRIDAY _____	_____ SATURDAY / SUNDAY _____

Notes: _____

Chapter
Six

Do Parents Feel They Are Truly Part of Your School Community Team?

Unity

I dreamed I stood in a studio
And watched two sculptors there.
The clay they used was a young child's mind,
And they fashioned it with care.
One was a teacher; the tools he used
Were books and music and art.
One a parent with a guiding hand,
And a gentle loving heart.
Day after day the teacher toiled,
With touch that was deft and sure,
While the parent labored by his side,
And polished and smoothed it over.
And when at last their task was done,
They were proud of what they had wrought.
For the things they had molded into the child
Could neither be sold nor bought.
And each agreed he would have failed
If he had worked alone.
For behind the parent stood the school,
And behind the teacher the home.

—Author Unknown

*D*ecember is a high-visibility month for your school and staff. There are numerous functions that involve your students. The winter concert is well attended and fully appreciated by your school community. Many principals invite grandparents and senior citizens to the last dress rehearsal. This holds down the crowd for the evening concert and also provides excellent public relations for your school. There are class parties that are enjoyable, but we recommend that each teacher submit a plan that includes a cleanup committee and the amount of class time involved. Restricting these events to one hour or an hour and a half makes more sense than having no time limit. Many principals allow parties only after the school day. If all children are involved in busing, this may prove impractical.

Three other popular activities are the book fair, the holiday gift shop, and visits to nursing homes. If the PTA hosts a book fair or a gift shop, it gives the principal an opportunity to make a statement about the kind of gifts parents should purchase. Presents such as books, stamp albums, rock collection kits, and science puzzles are more appropriate than pop culture items.

When we have students visit nursing homes or take up food collections for the needy, we are capturing the holiday spirit and enhancing our community service program. Most principals report that these initiatives often help to teach children the pleasure of giving, because so much of the holiday period is focused on receiving.

One admonition is to make certain that the academic tone is not replaced by a month of "party time." As staff members approach their own vacation periods, we should guard against their relaxing the school's primary mission. It is extremely difficult for them to focus on education when children are being pulled out for rehearsals by the chorus, orchestra, and band teachers. A word from you about expectations will help to maintain your educational tone.

Remember that the vacation period for teachers is not necessarily a holiday for your custodians. Establish some work objectives with your head custodian to be accomplished over the winter recess. If this is not done, you can be assured that you will return to find clean corridors and nothing else. This is an excellent time to do painting and classroom repair projects. Here, too, it's a matter of the principal's expectations.

One principal also has the secretarial staff be available for a few days during the vacation period. She organizes a work schedule that includes such tasks as the following:

1. Type diplomas or certificates.

2. Place certificates into individual folders unless they need teacher signatures.

3. Compose the principal's welcome-back letter to staff.

4. Write thank-you letters to all staff members who participated in holiday events.

5. Do the welcome-back weekly memorandum to highlight the coming events for January.

6. Organize the midyear report card materials.

You need a well-deserved vacation, but administrators must always address the following day's agenda. In this case, everything must be in place for the first day of the new year!

December's Key Tasks

Review Budget Proposals ✳

The cost of educating children in the United States increases every year. Work with the board of education by providing a clear and specific justification for each and every budget request. This can only happen with the cooperation, understanding, and hard work of the teachers and central office staff. Every budget request must be accompanied by the reasons it is needed. Items that will enhance the curriculum or assist in raising test scores are usually approved. Boards also look favorably on expenditures that address health and safety issues. Remember, increases in staffing must be justified, because personnel costs inflate budgets.

Personal Commentary/Notes: _____

_____

Holiday Work Schedule ✳

Take advantage of the holiday school closing to complete those projects that never seem to get finished. Work closely with the head custodian to make sure the priorities are addressed and that the building is ready for the new year.

Personal Commentary/Notes: _____

_____

Fire Drills ✳

Complete all reports due at the end of the calendar year. Use this as an opportunity to set goals to improve upon the past year's performance. Share the information with the appropriate staff and give recognition for jobs well done. Know your state and local requirements! In New York, 12 drills are required, of which 8 must be held prior to December 15, and the superintendent must be informed that the drills have been completed.

*Personal Commentary/Notes:*_____

_____

* *Faculty Meeting*

The December faculty meeting is a great time to celebrate with your staff. Using part of the meeting for a grab bag or some other holiday activity promotes staff spirit. Stress that the holiday school events should not detract from daily lessons and academic demands.

*Personal Commentary/Notes:*_____

_____

* *Classroom Observations*

All nontenured staff should have been observed at least once, preferably twice, by the end of December. This is especially important for those teachers whose rehiring is in question. Even though a central office chairperson may write a teacher's evaluation, the principal is expected to make the hiring recommendation. Having completed one or more firsthand observations of such a teacher gives the principal far more credibility when questions arise. When in doubt, do not rehire!

*Personal Commentary/Notes:*_____

_____

* *Holiday or Variety Show*

Most schools hold some type of student variety show. Our concerts are usually well attended. Principals should share rehearsal schedules with their staff. Also, be sure to preview the acts to avoid inappropriate themes or mishandling of sensitive issues.

If some form of judging is involved, be sure to have a process that makes the selection of winners a fair one. We tend to believe this judging to be more appropriate for secondary schools.

*Personal Commentary/Notes:*_____

_____

December's Communications

PTA Presentation ✳

This is the time of year to begin planning the annual PTA faculty recognition lunch and traditional fund-raising events. Monitoring all of the club and organization plans will avoid duplication and conflicts over dates and events. The PTA should receive preference, because they represent all of the parents in the school.

We have found that our staff members appreciate PTA faculty recognition days. In many schools, parents prepare a buffet lunch for teachers to thank them for their efforts. The tone is cordial, and it brings out the "T" in PTA.

Personal Commentary/Notes: _____

_____

Board of Education Meeting ✳

Carefully review the board of education agenda each month to anticipate questions that may be asked and to secure the necessary backup information and materials that may be called for. Alert the superintendent to any issues you think may be raised from the floor, and be prepared to respond in an appropriate and thoughtful way. Quick thinking and preparation on the part of the principal often prevent questions and concerns from becoming problems.

Complaints that are aired at PTA meetings will come to the board of education if the principal does not resolve them at his or her level. A respectful relationship with the PTA will help to resolve most issues at the building level.

Personal Commentary/Notes: _____

_____

Prepare for Retirement Parties ✳

This was an interesting addition for a December communication. A principal from Minnesota feels that his teachers should have a grand send-off after 35 years in the profession. He considers December as "down time" because all of the activities are so well planned by his music staff and PTA.

He writes letters to public officials requesting an acknowledgment of the service rendered by each individual retiree. (See Resource J—Request for Retirement Congratulatory Letter.)

He also starts planning the June event by eliciting the help of faculty volunteers to form a retirement committee. They decide the place, cost, and the emcee.

Personal Commentary/Notes: _____

_____

December's Planning

* Standardized Test Results

Prepare to mail home a copy of the results to each parent. An accompanying letter should help to interpret the scores and will instruct parents to refer any questions to the classroom teacher. Each state has different grade-level standardized examinations. One certainty is that in this present assessment era, there will be more rather than less testing!

*Personal Commentary/Notes:*_____

_____

* Winter Concert Schedule

Monitor the December calendar carefully. It quickly fills up, and conflicts with other schools and community-wide events should be avoided if at all possible. Also review the program for the music concert for appropriateness and length. As school music programs expand, some schools hold two winter concerts to avoid the long nights. Reminding parents of proper etiquette in your monthly letter will help make concerts a pleasant affair for all involved. Many times, the size of your performing groups determines if you need more than one night or if you have to use a secondary school's auditorium to accommodate the crowd.

*Personal Commentary/Notes:*_____

_____

* Locker Cleanup

This is the time of year to schedule hall-locker cleanup days. Coordinate with the custodians to provide extra trash cans in the halls. Ask teachers to check lockers to avoid problems later in the year. Many elementary schools have cubby space in each classroom. These should also be cleaned prior to the winter vacation.

*Personal Commentary/Notes:*_____

_____

December's Personnel

* Gifts

Principals often purchase gifts for secretaries and custodial staff during the holiday season. Be sure to coordinate this with the other staff members so that feelings are not hurt and so that gift giving does not get out of hand. Some schools provide food and refreshments to the entire secretarial and custodial staff rather than purchasing individual gifts. Other schools use this as an opportunity to make contributions to a charity in the name of the secretaries and custodians. We recommend some form of recognition for those valuable members of your school family, but we believe your school's "culture" should determine the form of acknowledgment to be instituted.

Personal Commentary/Notes: _____

_____

After-School Club Activities ✳

Every staff member who directs an extracurricular activity should receive a brief evaluation. This is also the time to hire for the second half of the year. Be consistent with school district and contractual guidelines.

Personal Commentary/Notes: _____

_____

December's Checklists

December's Key Tasks and Reminders

Major Assignments	Date Started	Date Completed	Days on Task
Review budget proposals			
Meet with head custodian to plan holiday work schedule			
Complete and report calendar-year fire drills			
Schedule faculty meeting			
Schedule classroom observations			
Preview holiday or variety show			

December's Communications Checklist

✔	Assignment
	Prepare PTA presentation
	Prepare a presentation for board of education meeting
	Prepare for retirement parties

December's Planning Checklist

✔	Assignment
	Prepare standardized test results
	Review winter concert schedule
	Set up midyear hall-locker cleanup days

December's Personnel Checklist

✔	Finalize
	Coordinate purchase of gifts for office and custodial staff
	Review extracurricular activities and their advisers

DECEMBER CALENDAR

MONTH: DECEMBER

YEAR: ____

MONDAY	TUESDAY	WEDNESDAY	THURSDAY	FRIDAY	SATURDAY / SUNDAY

Notes: ____

Chapter Seven

Do You Make New Year's Resolutions?

Ten Commandments for the
Humane Administrator

1. *Do not rebuke or correct any teacher in the presence of students or any other persons.*

2. *Praise teachers, and in the fields of their special preparation walk humbly.*

3. *Deal not lightly with any person's problem, but treat it as if it were your own.*

4. *Forget not the days of your youth. Keep a sense of humor.*

5. *Honor your custodians and your teachers, that your days may be long in the job that the school board has given you.*

6. *Let no child be judged by his behavior alone, but seek the causes of such behavior that they may be corrected.*

7. *Strive to see each child through the eyes of his parents and treat that child with love as if it were your own.*

8. *When you have a teacher who is old in the service, deal with him tenderly and understandingly. (Teachers do grow older, and they don't just fade away.)*

9. *Be sensitive to the needs of your whole community and have faith in its people, for in that faith you will find your strength.*

10. *Have a vision as well as devotion, that you might use all your talents for the benefit of all humanity.*

*T*he vacation period is over, and the building principal should reestablish a businesslike set of expectations for the staff and the student body. A tone-setting welcome-back presentation via the public address system and visits to classrooms are techniques often employed by school leaders for this purpose. Reminding students that this is the end of the first half of the academic year and urging them to prepare for examinations and assessment exams provides a clear, demanding, yet caring message.

The principal should be organizing both the end-of-first-semester activities and improving the second-semester schedules and staffing. This is an excellent example of how an administrator must operate in the present while always remaining cognizant of the forthcoming month, semester, plans, and activities. As we have stressed, the key tasks are critical to a principal's success. Caring and intent are admirable, but these alone will not achieve a functional environment without intense planning.

We would recommend a system to ensure that all staff evaluations are completed in a timely fashion. By now, the principal and other members of the supervisory staff should be able to list the teachers whose professional performance is in need of improvement. In the following two to three months, constructive plans should be offered to assist these teachers. If they are not to be retained, principals should know about these intentions in January and should be fully aware of the supervisory plans being developed. In this manner, there should be no surprises, and teachers should be informed prior to the spring recess if they are not to be retained. Many districts have contractual language that must be adhered to or else grievances will be filed.

Many schools have parent conferences at this time. The first open house was to discuss the curriculum and to review each teacher's expectations for the course and the students enrolled. This second conference is designed to review individual progress with the student's parent or guardian. We have no quarrel if the conference is held in November, December, January, or February. However, parents have a right to be fully informed by midyear, particularly if their child is having academic or behavioral problems. We must do more than just pay lip service to teacher-parent collaboration. More important, a conference minimizes the possibility that parents will feel they were not adequately informed that their child was in jeopardy of failing. Planning conferences, interim reports, and phone calls must eliminate this possibility. In the event that a child is not doing well, we must be proactive.

January's Key Tasks

∗ Review Evaluations

The midyear point is an important time to review staff performance and the evaluations of other supervisors. Meeting individually with each nontenured teacher provides an opportunity to build on the teacher's strengths and address any concerns. Frequent communication with all evaluators is critical in this area. If you have any doubts about a new or experienced staff member, notify the superintendent or your supervisor immediately. Members of the central office can also observe the staff member and offer suggestions. Don't give your superintendent a last-minute surprise.

*Personal Commentary/Notes:*_____

_____

∗ Remedial Plans

All teachers identified as needing improvement should have a remedial improvement plan developed. This plan should conform to appropriate union contract provisions. Providing release time for such teachers to observe colleagues and to attend training programs should be a part of all such plans. Utilizing staff mentors is a current practice that we support. Often local unions will help in this process instead of taking an adversarial position.

*Personal Commentary/Notes:*_____

_____

∗ Midyear Report Cards

The end of January is elementary report card time. An interesting idea is to ask teachers if they would like the principal to distribute report cards to the children. It is amazing how many teachers enjoy the practice. Principals need to schedule about 20 minutes per class to accomplish this activity. During the distribution, a brief pep talk is given to students. Then, in a dignified manner, which children take very seriously, the principal calls each child's name and shakes his or her hand. A reminder is given that the handshake is a sign that the student will continue to put forth his or her best effort. If such effort wasn't the case up to this point, it will certainly be a priority from now on!

*Personal Commentary/Notes:*_____

_____

Goal Review ✳

Meet with each chairperson or grade-level teacher-in-charge to review progress on goals for the year. Goals should be specific and driven by student achievement data. Limit the number of goals, because too many often means that little of substance is accomplished. In addition, the goals should fit into the overall school context and philosophy, for which the principal is responsible for establishing, promoting, and monitoring.

Personal Commentary/Notes: _____

_____

Curriculum Initiatives ✳

New course proposals and course revisions should be submitted to the superintendent and the board of education for approval, because the budget scheduling cycle for the coming year is about to begin. Principals are responsible for an ongoing process of curriculum evaluation and assessment in each discipline and grade level. The principal must make sure that all appropriate regulations and policies are followed. When you have no other administrators or supervisors to help, this becomes an awesome responsibility. We recommend networking with other district principals and high school chairpersons and directors to gain a broader perspective.

Personal Commentary/Notes: _____

_____

Finalize Budget ✳

Budget requests for the coming year should be finalized this month or in February. Begin planning for the presentation to the board of education and community. Many principals use computer-generated presentations to demonstrate the many uses of technology and to present their building's academic and physical plant needs. We have said that the greater the urgency for the request, the more likely it will be approved. We recommend going into your budget hearing with a detailed game plan.

Personal Commentary/Notes: _____

_____

Informal Class Visits ✳

Visibility among staff and students is a must for an effective principal. Build time into the daily schedule to informally visit classes. Keep a checklist of teach-

·ers visited to ensure that each is seen. In a small elementary school, we feel that a principal can stop by almost every class on a daily basis.

*Personal Commentary/Notes:*_____

_____

✳ *Faculty Meeting*

Most states require a variety of annual staff training sessions, and many include requirements for reviewing important safety and health procedures. Use a portion of each faculty meeting to meet this requirement. Local and regional offices are often willing to provide speakers, materials, or both to satisfy such training requirements. Typically such training is in the area of right-to-know, sexual harassment, security, and safety procedures. School nurses, social workers, and psychologists are valuable resources whom we believe are often underutilized in this regard.

*Personal Commentary/Notes:*_____

_____

✳ *Faculty Inservice*

This is a good time to revisit some classroom accommodations for specific behavior often connected with attention deficit disorders; these accommodations can also be applied to other less pervasive disorders. A principal from an Anchorage, Alaska, school district sent this instructive material to us. The authors believe that this material provides many excellent ideas for all of us, particularly in this era of inclusion. (See Resource K—Attention Deficit Disorder.)

*Personal Commentary/Notes:*_____

_____

January's Communications

✳ *Parent-Teacher Conferences*

Given the push to increase standards and the reexamination of social promotions, regular meetings between parents and teachers are becoming even more important. Designing the school schedule to include at least one or two parent-teacher conference days enhances communication. The principal is responsible for creating a schedule that is workable for both parents and teachers as well as articulating the purpose and function of the conference itself.

In elementary schools, many conferences for kindergartners and primary-grade students are arranged by having half-day school sessions. These day conferences are difficult for working parents and single-parent homes. Know your own community and plan to meet the needs of your school's parents.

Personal Commentary/Notes: _____

_____

PTA Presentation ✳

This is the opportune time of year to present program changes and enhancements proposed for the coming year. Parents can, and should be, the school's strongest supporters. The list of topics for elementary PTA meetings is endless. Some of the most popular themes include

✳ Interpreting standardized test scores

✳ Health and safety

✳ Reading your child's report card

✳ Homework, study time, and student projects

✳ The school budget and the building's needs

We particularly recommend a parent-child activity night in conjunction with the physical education curriculum. Our physical education teachers plan three separate evenings of fun—one evening each for K-1, 2-3, and 4-5. Each session lasts only one hour. During these evenings, children show off the many skills they have learned throughout the year. Then, in a spirit of fun, parents are invited to join their children in various activities. It always creates great family excitement to play "Cat and Mouse," to ride a scooter and play tag, or to enjoy a playful game of volleyball.

Personal Commentary/Notes: _____

_____

Board of Education Meeting ✳

Use this month's board of education meeting to highlight programs and departments that often receive little attention, such as art, music, physical education, library, and special education. Most parents and board members know little about the elementary programs that are available to students. Board members usually emphasize high school activities. This is your opportunity to give equal time to our K-5 program and students. It's a good time to give a "state of the school" outline, highlighting student and faculty accomplishments, fulfillment of annual goals, and projections for the upcoming year.

Always a powerful idea: Invite students to demonstrate accomplishments such as use of technology, products of math-science-technology units of study, and particular writing skills.

*Personal Commentary/Notes:*_____

_____

* **Lunch Program**

Asking students for feedback on the quality of the school lunch program and for suggestions is a great way to involve students and improve services for them. Many schools have established salad bars and health meals as a way of engaging students in the life of the school and making them more diet conscious. This also makes our lunchroom menu more consistent with our health curriculum.

*Personal Commentary/Notes:*_____

_____

January's Planning

* **Grants**

Many grants are available to supplement existing programs and to initiate new programs. Be sure to monitor grant deadlines to be certain that all available resources are utilized. Network with area principals to learn about new opportunities. Check out grants for before- and after-school child care programs, peer mediation, and multicultural initiatives.

*Personal Commentary/Notes:*_____

_____

January's Personnel

Staff Needs ✳

Make final recommendations for staffing needs for the coming year. Recommendations should be based on enrollment, curriculum needs, and individual and group test results. Begin to gear up for the staff recruitment and interview process. Teacher shortages in some urban and rural communities indicate that this recruitment process should start earlier.

Personal Commentary/Notes: _____

_____

Complete Nontenured ✳ *Teacher Evaluations*

All required teacher evaluations, especially for nontenured teachers, should have been completed and sent to the superintendent. Highlight those that indicate a problem or exemplary performance. By this time of the year, principals should have a good idea of each new teacher's progress. If not, additional observations should be scheduled immediately. A good question to ask yourself is "Will this teacher be a valuable addition to my staff?"

Personal Commentary/Notes: _____

_____

Complete Nonprofessional ✳ *Midyear Evaluations*

The principal must also oversee the evaluation of secretaries, custodians, monitors, aides, and so forth. Evaluations should be completed in a timely manner. The support staff is a critical part of any school's operation. Many of us forget that civil service staff members receive permanent status in just a few months. In a sense, they too have tenure. This is one reason to evaluate early and often!

Personal Commentary/Notes: _____

_____

January's Checklists

January's Key Tasks and Reminders

Major Assignments	Date Started	Date Completed	Days on Task
Review staff performance evaluations			
Create remedial plans for staff in need of improvement			
Distribute midyear report cards			
Review teacher progress on goals			
Review each department's progress on curriculum initiatives			
Finalize budget requests			
Make informal class visits			
Conduct faculty meeting			
Conduct faculty inservice			

January's Communications Checklist

✔	Assignment
	Conduct parent-teacher conferences
	Coordinate PTA presentation
	Prepare for board of education meeting
	Get feedback on school lunch program

January's Planning Checklist

✔	Assignment
	Review ongoing grants to ensure that all deadlines are met

January's Personnel Checklist

✔	Finalize
	Finalize staff needs for next semester
	Send superintendent all first-semester teacher evaluations
	Complete nonprofessional staff evaluations

JANUARY CALENDAR

MONTH: JANUARY

YEAR: _____

MONDAY ___	TUESDAY ___	WEDNESDAY ___	THURSDAY	FRIDAY ___	___ SATURDAY / SUNDAY ___
MONDAY ___	TUESDAY ___	WEDNESDAY ___	THURSDAY	FRIDAY	___ SATURDAY / SUNDAY ___
MONDAY ___	TUESDAY ___	WEDNESDAY ___	THURSDAY	FRIDAY ___	___ SATURDAY / SUNDAY ___
MONDAY ___	TUESDAY ___	WEDNESDAY ___	THURSDAY	FRIDAY ___	___ SATURDAY / SUNDAY ___
MONDAY ___	TUESDAY ___	WEDNESDAY ___	THURSDAY	FRIDAY ___	___ SATURDAY / SUNDAY ___

Notes: _____

Chapter Eight

February

When You Evaluate Your Staff, Do You Settle for a Bland Product?

You spoke to me of love
And I doubted you
You spoke to me of caring
And I doubted you
You spoke to me of my good worth
And I doubted you
You came to visit me in the hospital
And I believed every word you said.

—Robert Ricken

The second semester for elementary schools does not require the degree of change that it does for our secondary school colleagues. They must deal with new courses, dramatic changes in many teachers' schedules, and, in some cases, finals and midyear examinations. For us, it is imperative that the halfway mark in our school year isn't associated with a decline in enthusiasm. We recommend a thank-you note to the staff for their first half-year of effort and an inspirational speech at the first faculty meeting to address the five-month calendar ahead. We are probably facing state assessments in a few months, as well as culminating

Although you may have noticed the frequency with which we mention new teacher evaluations, we will continue to make this reminder. In most districts with strong union contracts, teachers must be informed as early as April if they are not being invited back. If you have doubts about any probationary employee, you are obligated to inform central office administration and district directors of special areas. Ideally, you'll all be comfortable, because you will have similar evaluations of the employee. If not, additional observations should be held immediately, and once again the central office should be informed. In many districts, the assistant superintendent for personnel will make an additional observation to help with the decision-making process.

Some school districts, particularly in cold climates, have begun to take a week off during the President's Day celebration. This not only saves the cost of fuel but also allows the custodial staff to clean the building and perform maintenance projects. It is a plan worth considering.

This might be a good time to review the status of all students in special education. A brief examination of each IEP (Individual Educational Plan) will prevent end-of-the-year surprises. Doing this usually helps to avoid costly independent hearings and the associated legal fees. Finally, you want to be sure that your staff is providing a quality program for this part of your school population.

February's Key Tasks

* Nontenured Teacher Evaluations

Be sure to meet all deadlines and procedural requirements in completing nontenured teacher evaluations. Far too many decisions not to rehire are reversed because of procedural flaws. Give teachers in difficulty the opportunity to resign rather than go through the termination process. We want to stress that if any doubt about a teacher's competence remains after the three-year probationary period, we unanimously recommend dismissal.

*Personal Commentary/Notes:*_____

_____

* Semester Transition

Review all class sizes, teaching assignments, and program changes once the new semester has started. Some sections become either very small or very large because of schedule changes or because of the special education inclusion process implemented during the first semester. Work with the grade-level staff to balance class sizes.

Personal Commentary/Notes: _____

_____

Master Schedule ✷

A well-conceived master schedule will provide both students and staff with the best possible program. Extensive preparation and planning is necessary to make this a reality. Begin working with key personnel to develop the upcoming master schedule. Many elementary principals now utilize the help and input of staff and administrative interns to create the new schedule; this also serves to demonstrate that scheduling is a complex and serious process.

Personal Commentary/Notes: _____

_____

Faculty Meeting ✷

Every faculty meeting should provide some open time for faculty questions, concerns, and announcements. Place a firm time limit on this part of the agenda, or it may dominate the entire meeting. Work behind the scenes to encourage faculty to bring issues forward, even if you do not agree with them. Dialogue helps air frustrations and sometimes generates creative solutions to problems. However, if the substance of the session can be covered in a memorandum, don't hold the meeting!

Personal Commentary/Notes: _____

_____

Report Cards ✷

By now the second-quarter report cards should have been issued. Most report card formats provide room for a message from the school. Make use of this opportunity to remind parents of important upcoming events. The report card should also contain a grading key or explanation at the bottom as well as a school phone number to call if parents sense a mistake. Recent changes in elementary report cards have enhanced the school-parent communication process. We recommend that every elementary principal maintain a file on other school districts' report cards. It might be appropriate to have a report card committee to review this vital communication device.

Personal Commentary/Notes: _____

_____

* *Grade Review*

Use the review of grades by teacher and department to identify areas of concern. Contact teachers with unusually high failure rates and offer assistance, if appropriate. Keep the records on file and compare on a year-to-year basis. If many students need improvement, the principal may want to ask the teacher what strategies he or she is using to help weaker students. A principal's suggestions may enhance the supervisory process.

*Personal Commentary/Notes:*_____

_____

February's Communications

* *Midyear Conferences*

Meet with the key teachers of each grade level and department to review end-of-the-year culminating activities, field days, science fairs, art shows, concerts, and field trips. Involve the PTA if chaperones are necessary, and ask homeroom teachers to ask for class mothers or fathers to serve as volunteers.

This is also the time to check your present budget to review expenditures and to be certain your supply codes have enough funds to carry you through the rest of the year. You might want to invite curriculum chairpersons and assistant superintendents to meet with your staff to begin planning summer writing projects. Contemporary changes in assessments and grade-level demands necessitate a constant realignment of your school's curriculum. This should be done in the summer, because it's too demanding to do during the school year.

*Personal Commentary/Notes:*_____

_____

* *PTA Presentation*

Work with the PTA leadership to prepare for PTA officer elections and end-of-the-year events. It is a good practice to review the PTA bylaws on an annual basis to avoid any possible controversies. Remember to report to your PTA regularly about the budget process, summer school plans, curriculum projects, and the progress of shared-decision-making teams.

*Personal Commentary/Notes:*_____

_____

Board of Education ✻

Use the board of education meeting to share the special science and math research projects many of your students have used to enter local, state, and national competitions. Involve the students in the presentations, encouraging them to engage the board members and audience directly. Don't allow board meetings to be dominated each month by high school happenings.

Personal Commentary/Notes: _____

_____

Government Letters ✻

Write to local elected officials for letters of congratulations to members of the fifth or sixth grade who are moving up to the middle school. These letters make a great handout at the end-of-the-year awards ceremony and serve as a great motivation for secondary school success. It's also a valuable public relations item. Parents are usually pleased and will remain part of your school's support system.

Personal Commentary/Notes: _____

_____

Schedule Conferences ✻

Encourage teachers to call or schedule conferences with parents of students who are doing poorly, who are not behaving well, or whose work habits have suddenly changed. These meetings can usually avoid more unpleasant conferences in the late spring. Positive changes should be reported as well, because these accolades are very much appreciated by parents and motivate students to try even harder.

Personal Commentary/Notes: _____

_____

Honor Roll ✻

Make it an annual practice to send students earning all *A*s or outstanding grades a letter of congratulation each marking period. Parents love saving these letters, and students often make them a part of their elementary school memories file.

Personal Commentary/Notes: _____

_____

February's Planning

✳ Supplies

Monitoring the status of school supplies on a regular basis prevents shortages from developing. Efficient record keeping will make the yearly budget request for supplies easier to justify and support. Many schools have begun to make purchases in bulk by joining educational cooperatives.

*Personal Commentary/Notes:*_____

_____

✳ Scheduling Input

Staff, assistant principals, and department chairpersons play a key role in determining teacher and student schedules. Their input must come early and often during the scheduling process. Cooperation and advance planning will minimize problems and place teachers in optimal assignments. Have teachers list the names of students who should be separated the following year.

*Personal Commentary/Notes:*_____

_____

✳ Facilities and Grounds

With the arrival of spring just around the corner, it is time to meet with the director of building and grounds to plan for the start of outdoor activities. An ongoing system of field maintenance and improvement will ensure that all children have a safe and appropriate place to play. Always check your playgrounds, because community children use them after school hours. One morning job for a building custodian should be to police the entire playground before the start of the school day!

*Personal Commentary/Notes:*_____

_____

February's Personnel

New Teacher Orientation ✳

This is a good time of year to look back and assess the new teacher orientation program. A survey of new teacher experiences will help in designing improvements to the process. As we mentioned previously, this should be done anonymously to ensure honest results and meaningful recommendations.

Personal Commentary/Notes: _____

_____

Support Staff ✳

Regular meetings with the support staff will keep the office running smoothly. Look for opportunities to give secretaries and custodians public compliments and a few hours of personal attention before the end-of-the-year rush begins. We recommend midyear evaluations for everyone, not just teachers.

Personal Commentary/Notes: _____

_____

February's Checklists

February's Key Tasks and Reminders

Major Assignments	Date Started	Date Completed	Days on Task
Complete evaluations of nontenured staff members			
Evaluate the second-semester schedule and program changeover process			
Meet with key personnel about next year's master schedule			
Plan monthly faculty meeting			
Issue second marking period report cards			
Review teacher and departmental grades			

February's Communications Checklist

✔	Assignment
	Hold midyear conferences with grade-level teachers-in-charge
	Prepare PTA presentation
	Prepare board of education report
	Write local government officials requesting letters of congratulation for graduates
	Encourage teachers to schedule parent conferences
	Generate honor roll congratulatory letters

February's Planning Checklist

✔	Assignment
	Check on status of school supplies
	Establish due dates for chairpersons' scheduling input
	Coordinate preparation of facilities and school grounds for spring sports

February's Personnel Checklist

✔	Finalize
	Evaluate new teacher orientation program
	Develop a dialogue with support staff

FEBRUARY CALENDAR

MONTH: FEBRUARY

YEAR: _____

MONDAY	TUESDAY	WEDNESDAY	THURSDAY	FRIDAY	SATURDAY / SUNDAY

Notes: _____

Chapter Nine

Are You Satisfied With the Tone of Your Building?

Definitions You Should Remember

The great sin, fear.
The most certain thing in life, change.
The greatest mistake, giving up.
The greatest joy, being needed.
The most satisfying experience, doing your duty first.
The greatest opportunity, the next one.
The greatest victory, victory over self.
The best action, keeping the mind clear and the judgment good.
The best play, successful work.
The greatest handicap, egotism.
The greatest blessing, good health.
The most expensive indulgence, hate.
The biggest fool, the man who lies to himself.
The greatest loss, loss of self-confidence.
The greatest gamble, substituting hope for facts.

When people are in an atmosphere of trust, they'll put themselves at risk;
Only through risk is there growth . . . reward . . . self-confidence . . . leadership.
—Author Unknown

March is usually free of holidays and thus has a full school calendar of approximately 21 to 23 days. If we look forward to April, there will be a spring recess. In May, we have the Memorial Day long weekend and in June, an abbreviated month because of the start of the summer vacation. March is thus obviously a month of intense school time and a period in which the creative administrator must balance education and culminating plans.

Teacher shortages, especially in special areas, require attention to both the rehiring process and the district's interviewing procedures. We strongly recommend that principals complete the supervision of new teachers and make decisions as early as possible about rehiring. This will enable the district to advertise in March or April in order to select the best available candidates for the following year. If you don't view this as a competitive situation, you are doomed to interview those who have been rejected by adjoining school districts. If you peruse the teacher want ads in June, July, and August, you can readily identify the districts with inferior hiring procedures.

Remind staff that we are quickly approaching the end of the third marking period. Teachers should bring to the principal's attention the names of students who are doing poorly and possibly need additional services. With standardized testing and state assessments on the horizon, this type of planning may avoid poor schoolwide academic results. This is an additional elementary-level tension that was at one time reserved for our secondary administrators. Most elementary scores are now published in the local press, and school comparisons are a reality. Unhappily, today's focus on education has made drill and practice a necessity.

March is an excellent time to plan a major schoolwide event directed at meeting a major curriculum objective. A science fair or a multicultural event can serve both the academic need and the desire to bring together the entire school community. This could be a joint goal of the PTA and the site-based committee. Most assessments today require children to do some form of research, interpret data, and write a coherent paragraph. All of these skills can be incorporated into one activity. The attendance of parents and community members is another positive benefit.

As we approach the last third of the school year, there are a few other areas that will be detailed under our Key Tasks for March:

* Make summer school plans and recommendations.

* Start pre-K screening.

* Plan field day or Olympics.

* Finalize budget requests.

* Decide which curriculum-writing projects you will recommend.

* Prepare the outside of the building for more frequent student use.

March's Key Tasks

Master Schedule ✳

Elementary principals are beginning to need many of the skills once required only of their secondary colleagues as they address the complexity of the master schedule. Elementary academic demands have necessitated more creativity with grouping of grade levels to enhance educational opportunities and increase the performance results of students. Teachers are no longer allowed to work in a closed-door environment, aloof from contact with their colleagues. We must also educate parents, because they often refer to the "good old days" when they were in elementary school. We have included in the resources a letter sent to parents describing parallel block scheduling. Although this was sent in September, we feel the content and informative style can be used by principals at any time for parental inservice. (See Resource L—Parallel Block Scheduling.)

Personal Commentary/Notes: _____

_____

Pre-K Screening ✳

This is the time to review the pre-K screening program. A grade-level meeting with your present kindergarten staff should be held to ascertain items that should be included or eliminated from the screening process. Special education teachers, speech therapists, social workers, psychologists, and physical education staff members should also be involved in the process.

Personal Commentary/Notes: _____

_____

Defending the Budget ✳

The principal must be the advocate for his or her budget requests, even though the work to identify the needs of the building was probably a group effort. Putting every request in priority order is essential, because we find that requests that are not funded in one year often receive support in the following year's budgetary process. Frequently, elementary principals are called in together to discuss the K-5 budget. We frown upon this, because the individual principal is entitled to equal time with his or her central office superior, as is usually afforded to the principals of secondary schools. If this last meeting is with the superintendent, it is extremely advantageous to present your building's needs to him or her directly.

A passionate presentation often receives the endorsement of the superintendent. The support of the "boss" will help guarantee a thorough presentation to the board of education. Your conversation should also provide the superintendent with a host of reasons why each proposed project is vital to your school's educational program. Health and safety requests will usually receive the endorsement of the board of education if they are presented properly and with a sincere concern for the children.

*Personal Commentary/Notes:*_____

_____

* Evaluations

Using the evaluation process correctly is as important as the substance in any evaluation. Make sure that the staff member has received everything required in writing, and have a second administrator sit in on any meetings in which the teacher has a union representative present. Follow up each conference with a quick memo of record to the teacher, and put a copy in his or her personnel file.

As we have noted in the introduction to this month, the timing of evaluations is a paramount personnel concern. Your evaluations must

1. Conform to education law

2. Be consistent with the teacher's union contract

3. Be written to improve instruction and teacher performance

4. Document every area where you've noted unsatisfactory teacher performance

*Personal Commentary/Notes:*_____

_____

* Drills

Complete as many remaining fire and safety drills as possible to minimize class interruption during the final months of the school year.

*Personal Commentary/Notes:*_____

_____

* Faculty Meeting

Make sure to publish an agenda for each meeting at least a week in advance. Don't hold the meeting just to say you had the meeting. Busy faculty will appreciate your recognition of the time demands they face. As stated previously, it is better to cancel a meeting than to fill the time with material that could be shared through a simple memo. This is a good time to review the calendar of activities for April, May, and June. There should be no surprises for your staff, and every class should fully participate in all special events.

Personal Commentary/Notes: _____

_____

School Recognition Program ✳

There are both state and national elementary school recognition programs. Applications for these require progress reports, and the process is often its own reward. The self-examination required by your staff and the scrutiny of your programs will be beneficial whether you win "recognition" or not. Hint: Check with your superintendent prior to motivating your staff, because some districts do not want to set up competition between their elementary schools.

Personal Commentary/Notes: _____

_____

March's Communications

Summer Curriculum ✳

Most districts provide funding and time for staff to revise and create new curricula over the summer. The principal should coordinate proposals for such projects, prioritize them, and submit them to the superintendent for approval. This is another excellent item for faculty meetings or site-based committees. Teachers usually know best what areas will benefit from improved curriculum designs.

Personal Commentary/Notes: _____

_____

Supervising Closing Activities ✳

The end of the school year is one of the busiest times of the year for student activities and programs. Many faculty members will be needed to supervise the events. Give all faculty the opportunity for these positions, and create a schedule to ensure that every event is adequately staffed. Because remuneration is frequently involved, be sure to come up with an equitable plan. If there is contract language governing these assignments, be sure to adhere to the contract and avoid grievances.

Personal Commentary/Notes: _____

_____

* Board of Education

A presentation featuring the results of standardized testing is an annual expectation. Clear and comprehensive tables and graphs will help parents and the board of education to understand the strengths and areas in need of improvement. A handout with summary material is an important way to share the results. Tie the presentation into the need for summer school and summer curriculum-writing projects. Any problems with test data results should be accompanied by proposed solutions. Informing the public that your staff conducted an item analysis and is determined to stress weak areas in next year's curriculum demonstrates that you've done your homework.

*Personal Commentary/Notes:*_____

_____

* PTA Meeting

Each year the PTA raises funds to support the school program. Keep a list of materials, equipment, and special items to suggest when the association leaders ask what the school would like. Be sure to publicly thank the PTA for the contribution and their ongoing efforts in support of the school. Items that are not included in the district budget should be part of your PTA "wish list." Principals have reported a host of projects funded by the PTA, and many labor-intensive paintings and hall murals were completed by parents and former graduates.

*Personal Commentary/Notes:*_____

_____

March's Planning

* Orientation Programs for Middle School

Cooperate with the middle school counseling staff, because they are attempting to provide an orderly transition to the middle school. Make certain that these activities do not disrupt your program. Communication between you and the middle school staff is the key to a beneficial orientation program.

*Personal Commentary/Notes:*_____

_____

* Summer School

More and more students are being required to attend summer programs as standards are raised. The summer school course bulletin should be completed and prepared so that appropriate staffing and materials can be secured. This has suddenly become a critical component of our elementary program. You should become intimately involved with the selection of the summer school's principal and staff. Unless guaranteed by the teacher contract, positions should go to the most qualified staff, not to those with the most seniority!

Personal Commentary/Notes: _____

_____

Closing Prep ✳

Closing school is a complicated and detail-laden process. Checklists for each department and a comprehensive teacher checkout sheet should be prepared at this time. No, it's not too early!

Personal Commentary/Notes: _____

_____

March's Personnel

Staff Recognition Lunch ✳

The PTA traditionally holds a staff recognition lunch. Be sure to allow everyone to attend, and write the appropriate thank-you notes on behalf of the faculty. These events are appreciated by your staff and make the terms *family* and *school community* a reality.

Personal Commentary/Notes: _____

_____

Cards and Notes ✳

Keep a supply of sympathy, get-well, congratulations, and thank-you cards on hand to send to staff on important occasions. Make sure your secretary keeps you up-to-date on social developments with the staff. We recommend that you always send condolence messages to parents and staff when any sad event occurs.

Personal Commentary/Notes: _____

_____

* *Hiring Process*

Begin the new teacher hiring process by advertising at colleges and in newspapers. Screen applications by committee and involve staff in the interview process. Invite semifinalists to teach a model lesson, and be sure to check references carefully. Often, what is not said in a reference is critical. Recommend finalists to the superintendent. A writing sample is also a valuable tool for the committee to consider.

Personal Commentary/Notes: _____

_____

March's Checklists

March's Key Tasks and Reminders

Major Assignment	Date Started	Date Completed	Days on Task
Begin work on master schedule			
Begin pre-K screening			
Prepare to defend budget recommendations			
Complete all nontenured teacher evaluations and recommendations			
Complete yearly fire and emergency drills			
Plan monthly faculty meeting			
Engage in recognition programs			

March's Communications Checklist

✔	Assignment
	Collect summer curriculum development requests
	Request names of teachers to supervise all closing activities
	Plan monthly board of education presentation
	Prepare PTA meeting presentation

March's Planning Checklist

✔	Assignment
	Coordinate middle school orientation program
	Complete the summer school bulletin with course options
	Revise the building-closing checklist and teacher checkout form
	Establish the scholarship and awards committee

March's Personnel Checklist

✔	Finalize
	Host the staff recognition day lunch
	Send cards or notes to staff for key events
	Begin new teacher hiring process

MARCH CALENDAR

MONTH: MARCH

YEAR: _____

MONDAY	TUESDAY	WEDNESDAY	THURSDAY	FRIDAY	SATURDAY / SUNDAY

Notes: _____

Chapter Ten

In Your Long-Range Plans, Are Teachers Part of the Solution?

Strategic Planning

Strategic planning is not an edict, but a consensus plan derived through the application of the basic principles of participative management, specifically,

1. *that those closest to the job know the job better than anyone else,*

2. *that strategic information flows downward and operational information flows upward,*

3. *that decisions should be made at the lowest possible level,*

4. *that one cannot participate outside of his or her level of authority, accountability, and information, and*

5. *that accountability is commensurate with authority.*

—William J. Cook

The third quarter of our school year ends during the month of April. We urge principals to guard against a holiday atmosphere, because there is much to do in order to prepare for the closing activities of May and June. One look at our key tasks indicates that teacher evaluations, budget, and the master schedule must be addressed as part of our plans for the next school year.

Most budgets are voted upon in May, and thus our best thinking should be presented for the superintendent's consideration at this time.

Most teacher contracts and state laws require May notification for nontenured teachers who will not be rehired.

Principals who wish to develop a more comprehensive master schedule should be discussing the benefits with the staff and parents in April.

Often we take advisers of student activities for granted. Such activities become a lower priority compared with all of the other issues we must confront. We believe that principals should give some thought to the effectiveness of the extracurricular program. Evaluate the performance of your staff, and don't allow seniority to blind your professional judgment. Often long-term activity advisers bring a degree of experience to the job, but they frequently lose their zest and creativity. An honest assessment of your staff and program is in order.

The same thought should be given to grade-level leaders. Don't allow your senior staff to continue in a position if they have retired on the job. Your younger and more enthusiastic teachers deserve the recognition and the opportunity for leadership. Ultimately, this is the pool of leadership from which you may some-day have the opportunity to select an assistant principal. We consider this a critical part of your staff development program.

We apologize if this item sounds like an exhortation, but that's exactly the way we feel. As principals, we know that the budget is being reviewed by our superintendent and the board of education. A personal presentation by a knowledgeable principal is the only way to minimize cuts to your proposed budget. Armed with specific reasons for each expenditure, the principal must be a convincing presenter. Districts have a habit of trivializing elementary budget items. Be a forceful advocate for your educational programs.

Spring concerts are usually held in April. Review the music with the teachers and leaders of the department. Remember, this is a great opportunity for your school and its staff to become highly visible to parents and community members. Check your bulletin boards and the entire facility in order to highlight the work of students and the educational atmosphere of your school.

April's Key Tasks

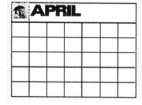

* Master Schedule

By this point in the year, next year's master schedule should be nearing completion. Be sure to check each teacher's schedule to see that all contract requirements have been met. Review class sizes and begin the balancing process. Check your grade-level teaching strength. Principals should switch teachers to different grade assignments as state assessments are targeted for new grade levels. Many principals are now utilizing *looping* so that strong staff members can remain with the same group of children for two years. The elementary master schedule now demands a new focus. The status quo won't work in an era of changing demands!

Personal Commentary/Notes: _____

_____

Leisure Time ✳

As educators, we have a responsibility to address many family and societal concerns. The National TV Turnoff Week is an excellent opportunity to support appropriate leisure-time activities. We can help parents monitor the overuse of television and become aware of more wholesome uses of leisure time. (See Resource M—National TV Turnoff Week.)

Personal Commentary/Notes: _____

_____

Moving-Up Exercises ✳

All materials and equipment for graduation should be ordered by now. Meet with the fifth-grade class officers to obtain their input on the program and the ceremony. Begin the process to identify student speakers and those who wish to perform a musical presentation at the program. One school permits any fifth grader to submit an essay to be read at graduation. A panel of faculty members selects the best essays to be part of the ceremony. Our event must not compete with the formality of a secondary school graduation. We should be planning an appropriate culmination for the K-5 experience. This should be a warm and relaxed assembly with a sincere farewell from the faculty and principal.

Personal Commentary/Notes: _____

_____

Budget Presentation ✳

The public budget presentation for the coming year should focus on how the instructional needs of all students will be met. Highlight new programs and expenses as well as savings and adjustments. Provide members of the audience with a one-page summary handout. Our introduction urges principals to come prepared with all backup material in order to lend support to their verbal presentation. A casual approach will cost you dearly.

Personal Commentary/Notes: _____

_____

✳ *Student Government*

Monitor the student government election process. Each candidate should receive a written set of guidelines and instructions for the election process as well as a statement of the responsibilities for the position. The student council adviser should preview all speeches. Many elementary schools hold elections later in the spring. We find that having the new council members observe the present year's officers organize the closing school events provides an excellent inservice program. The new student leaders will plan in the summer for the following year.

*Personal Commentary/Notes:*_____

_____

April's Communications

✳ *Testing Presentation*

The April PTA meeting is a good time to review the major end-of-the-year activities and expectations. Give parents guidelines and suggestions for managing the standardized testing pressures. Test anxiety is now experienced by parents as well as children. A letter outlining the mechanics of the testing process, which is ordinarily sent to teachers, might be shared with interested parents at such a meeting. We are unhappy with this latest testing and assessment trend, which is a national phenomena. However, when scores are published and comparisons are drawn, we naturally want to do well. The PTA presentation should specify what your staff is doing to maximize student performance and what parents can do to help at home. (See Resources N and O—Standardized Testing Memo to Teachers and Standardized Testing Letter to Parents.)

*Personal Commentary/Notes:*_____

_____

✳ *Board of Education Meeting*

This is an appropriate meeting to share recent school statistics. Provide the board with a five-year summary of results and the appropriate comparisons to other K-5 schools. Identify how the curriculum supports students in preparing for these examinations and demonstrate the school's commitment to helping all students. The data from your recent PTA meeting will help to make the presentation relevant. The superintendent and board should appreciate your faculty's strategies to reach out to parents to assist in maximizing test results. One school whose results were poor had the entire faculty involved in solving the problem.

Their personal input and team effort dramatically improved the following year's results. Testing is a team responsibility!

Personal Commentary/Notes: _____

_____

Letters *

Send out congratulation letters to students who earned all *As* (or *Os* for outstanding work) during the last report card period. Some schools also provide a special breakfast for these students in recognition of their achievement. Many principals also send notes to children who have demonstrated noticeable improvement in grades or behavior. Parents are extremely pleased with this type of correspondence.

Personal Commentary/Notes: _____

_____

Spring Musical *

The preparation and staging of a schoolwide musical or play takes months of work on the part of staff and students. Be sure to attend as many performances as possible and to send the director, staff, and performers a letter of commendation. Day and evening performances allow for the participation of working parents, grandparents, senior citizens, and local public officials.

Personal Commentary/Notes: _____

_____

Faculty Evaluations *

All probationary teacher observations required as part of the yearly evaluation process should be completed by the first part of April. Use the remainder of the month to write and review all teacher evaluations. Use the evaluation conference as an opportunity to seek feedback on your own work as principal. Most districts send out rehiring notices in May, and thus we urge principals to finish these observations early. The final evaluations for tenured staff members can wait until May or June.

Personal Commentary/Notes: _____

_____

Warning Letters *

Do an updated review of the academic status of each child and send letters to each student who may be required to attend summer school. In situations where it appears that there is no chance for the student to salvage the year, a parent conference to discuss retention should be held. This form of early notification prepares parents in case they have other summer plans, and it eliminates the potential for the argument that they had no idea their child was doing poorly. In the event you have a difficult parent, we recommend sending a registered letter!

*Personal Commentary/Notes:*_____

_____

✳ *Middle School*

Keep the parents of children going to the middle school apprised of the program through an annual orientation meeting. This is the responsibility of your middle school principal, but the successful transition should also be your concern. Middle school counselors should

1. Meet with your fifth-grade staff

2. Describe the middle school program to the students

3. Host a visit to the middle school for children during the day and parents at night

*Personal Commentary/Notes:*_____

_____

April's Planning

✳ *Vacation Schedules*

Develop a comprehensive calendar of summer work and vacation schedules for your administrative team and building secretaries. Be sure that someone is available in the building all summer or at least the last two weeks in August to answer questions and to register new students. Try to identify a few days when all administrators are available to hold summer planning meetings. In many elementary schools, the administrative staff is just the principal. In this case, simply coordinate your schedule with those of your secretary, aides, and head custodian.

*Personal Commentary/Notes:*_____

_____

Cultural Arts ✻

The spring is an excellent time to promote the arts program by sponsoring a community-wide cultural arts festival. Art students can display their best work, and drama and speech students can offer performances. Music presentations should include the regular student groups along with an opportunity for individual recitals. Sometimes grade-level performances can be based upon the curriculum, and the integration of the arts supports what is happening in the classroom. These performances can help with the retention of cognitive material.

Personal Commentary/Notes: _____

_____

Academic Awards ✻

An annual academic awards program should be held each year. The principal should review the program to ensure that as many students as possible receive some recognition. Service, attendance, and the arts should receive equal billing with academic accomplishments. The planning committee should begin its work now so that the assembly can be held during the last week or two of school. Most children treasure these awards even if they are in the form of a paper certificate.

Personal Commentary/Notes: _____

_____

April's Personnel

Teacher Openings ✻

Developing a substantial pool of quality applicants for teacher openings is becoming more and more difficult at this point in the year. Establishing and maintaining contacts with area teachers colleges and, if needed, sending staff to recruiting fairs are good techniques to secure the best possible candidates. Use both local and regional newspapers to place ads for the openings. Although many of these responsibilities are those of central office personnel, we recommend that principals take an assertive posture during the process. Don't forget your excellent student teachers and superior substitutes. You have an inside track on these candidates!

Personal Commentary/Notes: _____

_____

❋ *Secretary's Day*

The principal's position includes having a school secretary. Show just how important he or she is by making the celebration for Secretary's Day something special. If you are blessed with more than one secretary, honor those people as well. Teachers also appreciate the building's secretary and will generally be happy to be a part of the celebration.

*Personal Commentary/Notes:*_____

_____

April's Checklists

April's Key Tasks and Reminders

Major Assignments	Date Started	Date Completed	Days on Task
Complete draft of master schedule for coming year			
Encourage worthwhile leisure-time pursuits			
Prepare for moving-up exercises			
Make public presentation on proposed budget for elementary school			
Conduct election for student government officers			

April's Communications Checklist

✔	Assignment
	Update PTA on end-of-the-year activities and special testing
	Attend monthly board of education meeting
	Send letter of congratulations to students with all *As* in third marking period
	Congratulate cast and crew of spring musical
	Conduct faculty evaluations
	Contact parents of students in danger of not graduating
	Participate in middle school orientation program

April's Planning Checklist

✔	Assignment
	Establish summer vacation and work schedules for administrative team
	Facilitate planning program for cultural arts festival
	Develop program for annual academic awards assembly

April's Personnel Checklist

✔	Finalize
	Place advertisements for anticipated staff openings
	Celebrate Secretary's Day

APRIL CALENDAR

MONTH: APRIL _____

YEAR: _____

MONDAY ___	TUESDAY ___	WEDNESDAY ___	THURSDAY ___	FRIDAY ___	SATURDAY / SUNDAY ___
MONDAY ___	TUESDAY ___	WEDNESDAY ___	THURSDAY ___	FRIDAY ___	SATURDAY / SUNDAY ___
MONDAY ___	TUESDAY ___	WEDNESDAY ___	THURSDAY ___	FRIDAY ___	SATURDAY / SUNDAY ___
MONDAY ___	TUESDAY ___	WEDNESDAY ___	THURSDAY ___	FRIDAY ___	SATURDAY / SUNDAY ___
MONDAY ___	TUESDAY ___	WEDNESDAY ___	THURSDAY ___	FRIDAY ___	SATURDAY / SUNDAY ___

Notes: _____

Chapter Eleven

Do You Hire to Fill a Vacancy, or Do You Search for Excellent Candidates?

Why "Pretty Good" Isn't Good Enough

There once was a pretty good student
Who sat in a pretty good class,
And was taught by a pretty good teacher
Who always let pretty good pass.

He wasn't terrific at reading,
He wasn't a whiz bang at math,
But for him education was leading,
Straight down a pretty good path.

He didn't find school too exciting,
But he wanted to do pretty well,
And he did have some trouble with writing,
And nobody taught him to spell.

When doing arithmetic problems,
Pretty good was regarded as fine,
Five plus five needn't always add up to be ten,
A pretty good answer was nine.

The pretty good school that he went to,
Was there in a pretty good town,
And nobody there seemed to notice,
He could not tell a verb from a noun.

AUTHOR'S NOTE: Excerpt from "The Osgood File" used with permission of Charles Osgood.

The pretty good student in fact was,
Part of a pretty good mob,
And the first time he knew what he lacked was,
When he looked for a pretty good job.

It was then, when he sought a position,
He discovered that life could be tough,
And he soon had a sneaky suspicion,
Pretty good might not be good enough.

The pretty good town in our story,
Was part of a pretty good state,
Which had pretty good aspirations,
And prayed for a pretty good fate.

There once was a pretty good nation,
Pretty proud of the greatest it had,
Which learned much too late,
If you want to be great,
Pretty good is, in fact, pretty bad.

—The "Osgood File"

*T*he completion of all classroom observations of staff by the end of this month is necessary if final evaluations are to be given prior to the summer vacation as we recommended in April. As stated, we believe that evaluations of nontenured staff should be completed a month earlier. We always recommend that, as part of the teacher's final evaluation, a discussion about specific goals for the upcoming year should take place. Some districts actually formalize this process. The value is that staff members are aware of the goals if they wish to plan over the summer. Setting goals also allows for some inservice or college courses to be taken in July or August.

A complete review of the present year's budget is in order. Department chairpersons, teachers, and secretaries should be able to discuss each area's excess or shortfall. Ideally, this was already done several months earlier, while preparing the next school year's budget. However, we find the analysis at this time to be far more accurate for future planning.

If your district has the teaching staff involved in the hiring of their future colleagues, this process should be in full swing. Whenever possible, we recommend that all candidates teach a model lesson when they become semifinalists for a position. Staff members who participate in hiring new teachers not only learn from the interviews but also become proactive in helping the candidate when he or she joins the staff. Often the teacher who interviews candidates becomes a willing mentor.

The checklist of closing tasks becomes a massive clerical job. Signatures—of diplomas, award certificates, and student yearbooks—are in some cases legally necessary and in other cases are emotionally satisfying to your graduates. However, finalizing evaluations, making hiring recommendations, fine-tuning the master schedule, and ensuring the integrity of final assessments are essential to the evaluation of the present year and the start of the next. Addressing these enormous responsibilities is what makes elementary school principals special. An error in May can create chaos in September.

We have a final word about summer school, a new and growing responsibility for elementary principals. As you will see, this has become a key task for us. What was exclusively a part of the secondary principal's domain has become a critical area for study and implementation by the elementary principal.

May's Key Tasks

Summer School ✶

The national focus on education has become an issue in American politics. Negative press has directed attention toward every aspect of the educational profession. Those of us in elementary education were usually immune to the criticism. However, the recent emphasis on standards and assessments has forced us to take another look at many elementary school practices. One area that has received critical attention is the old process of social promotion. An ancillary concern has been the demand for specific promotional standards for each grade level.

Summer school is no longer a frill or a summer day camp alternative. The elementary principal is advised to become intimately involved in every aspect of the summer school, from the selection of the principal to the course selections and disciplinary procedures. We should be totally knowledgeable of how the results in summer school will be communicated to our staff. This is a growing responsibility that demands our full attention!

Personal Commentary/Notes: _____

_____

Faculty Meeting ✶

Faculty members are often tired and frustrated from a long school year. Plan to make the May faculty meeting an upbeat, fun experience. Engage faculty in an exercise that breaks from the routine and bureaucratic procedures. A poetry reading, a visit by graduates, or a PTA Thank-You Tea are activities that will be welcomed at this point in the year.

Personal Commentary/Notes: _____

_____

✱ *Evaluation of Administrators*

The evaluation of your administrative team should hold no surprises for anyone. Concerns should be addressed as they occur, and significant issues should be handled with frequent meetings and plans for improvement. Some principals have their assistant principals and grade-level leaders complete a self-evaluation as part of this process.

*Personal Commentary/Notes:*_____

_____

✱ *Report on Goals*

Each year your school has one or more goals and committees working on projects or standing issues. The principal should prepare a yearly report for the superintendent that identifies each goal and committee and summarizes the accomplishments of the year. This report often is incorporated into the evaluation of the principal by his or her supervisor. It is also the time to develop your goals for the upcoming year. Schoolwide objectives are also an excellent outcome of your site-based committee.

*Personal Commentary/Notes:*_____

_____

✱ *Fire Drills*

All required fire and safety drills should have been completed and the appropriate forms and reports submitted to the necessary parties. A year without any problems is an opportunity to recognize the fine work of the custodial and maintenance staff.

*Personal Commentary/Notes:*_____

_____

✱ *Exit Interviews*

Often the best source of information on the quality of the program and staff comes from the students themselves. Schedule time during this month to meet with individuals or with small groups of fifth graders to assess their experience. A follow-up written survey during the next year gives even more feedback about how well the students were prepared for the middle school. These results can make for a very lively faculty meeting discussion. Be sure to clear this activity with your union building representatives to avoid the appearance of "checking up" on the staff.

Personal Commentary/Notes: _____

_____

Graduation Certificates ✳

During May, it seems that the stack of certificates to sign just keeps getting larger. Use this time as an opportunity to think about each student as you sign his or her diploma or award certificates. How many do you know well? Finding that you do not know very many students should serve as a motivation to spend more time directly with students during the next school year.

Personal Commentary/Notes: _____

_____

Standardized Tests ✳

As the assessment movement affects more and more schools, May is often the time when standardized tests are required. Work with the faculty to devise the optimal testing environment, and adjust the school schedule of activities to give students as much preparation as possible in the days leading up to the testing. This has become a personal dilemma for most of us. The teachable moment has been relegated to second place. Subject content, drill, and practice have replaced the joy of learning. Nevertheless, we must deal with these new performance mandates!

Personal Commentary/Notes: _____

_____

District Budget Vote ✳

Typically, school districts hold their annual budget/school board elections in May. The school is often a major polling site for the vote. Be sure to follow all election rules, and provide the election volunteers with refreshments and administrative support. Smooth election procedures will help minimize controversy and problems.

Many elementary school principals have decided to host major events in their buildings on the day of the district's budget vote. This is a way to get large numbers of parents to come to the program and vote for the budget!

*Personal Commentary/Notes:*_____

_____

May's Communications

✳ Closing Procedures

The last days of the school year can be hectic and confusing if clear closing procedures have not been established and communicated. Work with the secretarial staff to design a sign-out process that avoids long lines and frustration. Make sure that all teachers provide you with a summer address. Many schools build a special fun faculty meeting into the last day as a closing activity. This is a great time to recognize staff who have made special contributions. Ending the year on a positive note will help everyone return in the fall, ready to start the year with enthusiasm. Plan in May; celebrate in June!

*Personal Commentary/Notes:*_____

_____

✳ PTA Meeting

Be sure to use one of the final PTA meetings of the year to publicly recognize the officers for their volunteer work and contributions to the school. Some principals keep a supply of school pins or T-shirts on hand to give as token gifts at such occasions. Many PTAs recognize teachers who have taken an active role in parent activities. Certificates, gifts, and letters of appreciation are given to teachers and secretaries.

*Personal Commentary/Notes:*_____

_____

✳ Progress Reports

Only secondary schools used to be concerned with failing students or "senioritis." In contemporary elementary schools, communication with parents has become a major part of our job and a critical teacher responsibility. Students who are doing poorly and not meeting standards must have their parents informed immediately. We've discussed this previously, but by May in the school calendar, we cannot afford to surprise a parent with a negative academic report. To ensure the cooperation of these families, we must alert them early to the problem and make several suggestions for helping the child. Tutoring, summer school, or more frequent reports from the classroom teacher may be recommended by the staff. The key is to review all students who are having learning problems and report this information to their families or guardians. Parents have a right to assume that no news indicates their child is doing satisfactory work!

Personal Commentary/Notes: _____

_____

May's Planning

Activities Calendar ✳

Developing the yearly activities calendar is a complicated task. A special meeting devoted to this job should be held with all cocurricular advisers. The calendar should also be coordinated with the middle school(s) and high school(s), because many parents have students at more than one school. Be sure to note the days before each marking period is scheduled to end and any special testing dates. A careful check of religious holidays will also avoid later problems. We would involve our PTA and all groups who use our buildings after school. Conflicts between Little League, scouting groups, and 4-H clubs can be avoided by meeting with their representatives in May or June.

Personal Commentary/Notes: _____

_____

Budget Analysis ✳

April or May is an excellent month to review the year's expenditures. Note areas where you have either overspent or not expended a lot of funds, and make the appropriate adjustments for the following year. Being proactive in this area will serve you well throughout the budget process.

Personal Commentary/Notes: _____

_____

✴ *Attendance at Spring Events*

The principal's calendar is often a logistical nightmare. Work with your secretary to block out certain times for class visits and for just wandering around the halls, and be sure to highlight all major evening and weekend activities. Although the principal does not have to attend every event, we should carefully avoid appearing to favor one type of activity over another.

Elementary principals are often invited to a host of end-of-the-year celebrations by community groups. The advice in the previous paragraph is sincere. Try to rotate your attendance, and always write notes of regret when your schedule does not permit your attendance.

*Personal Commentary/Notes:*_____

_____

✴ *School Pictures*

The principal must be the chief guardian of instructional time. Schedule activities such as fifth-grade portraits at a time when students are not in class. The faculty and parent community will respect and support this approach. They will also receive the important messages that school is still in session and that you expect teaching to remain the priority.

*Personal Commentary/Notes:*_____

_____

May's Personnel

✴ *Cocurricular Recommendations*

Finding appropriate staff to fill the many cocurricular positions each year can be a challenge. Be sure to give preference to your own teachers or those in the district. The teacher contract probably mandates this. An interview and evaluation process is just as important as when you hire a teacher. Completing your recommendations this month is important, because the final month of the year is far too busy to address this issue.

*Personal Commentary/Notes:*_____

_____

Cocurricular Report *

Require each cocurricular adviser to complete and submit an end-of-the-year report. This should include a list of meetings held, number and names of students involved, and major activities accomplished. A financial accounting should also be included.

Personal Commentary/Notes: _____

_____

Ongoing Teacher Hiring Process *

Most of the teacher openings for the coming year should be filled by now. Waiting until the summer makes it difficult, because many staff are not available to participate in the process. A detailed recommendation with at least two reference checks will assist the superintendent in presenting the candidates to the board of education. Make no mistake—we are competing for talented teachers. Starting early is one way to secure quality newcomers.

Personal Commentary/Notes: _____

_____

Staff Recognition *

Recognizing staff is an important part of the symbolic role a principal plays. The recognition should be genuine and should acknowledge all groups that work in the building. Sometimes principals defer this task to the PTA. The PTA program should augment your own. Your faculty needs to hear directly from you. A laudatory letter is our minimal expectation.

Personal Commentary/Notes: _____

_____

May's Checklists

May's Key Tasks and Reminders

Major Assignments	Date Started	Date Completed	Days on Task
Get involved with summer school planning			
Conduct monthly faculty meeting			
Complete evaluations of administrative team			
Prepare work on goal completion and committee work			
Conduct any remaining fire drills			
Complete exit interviews for upper grades			
Sign diplomas and award certificates			
Oversee administration of standardized tests			
Oversee the district budget vote			

May's Communications Checklist

✔	Assignment
	Complete and distribute school closing procedures
	Give monthly presentation to PTA meeting
	Distribute progress reports

May's Planning Checklist

✔	Assignment
	Begin developing activities calendar for the coming year
	Complete and analyze the present year's budget
	Plan to supervise and attend key spring events
	Coordinate scheduling and taking of school pictures

May's Personnel Checklist

✔	Finalize
	Submit recommendations for cocurricular appointments for next year
	Complete cocurricular enrollment/activity report
	Complete teacher hiring process
	Recognize faculty and staff for length of service and for retirement

MAY CALENDAR

MONTH: MAY

YEAR: _____

MONDAY	TUESDAY	WEDNESDAY	THURSDAY	FRIDAY	SATURDAY / SUNDAY
___	___	___	___	___	___
___	___	___	___	___	___
___	___	___	___	___	___
___	___	___	___	___	___
___	___	___	___	___	___

Notes: _____

Chapter Twelve

What Will Be Your Legacy?

To laugh often and much,
To win the respect of intelligent people,
And the affection of children,
To earn the appreciation of honest critics,
And endure the betrayal of false friends,
To appreciate beauty,
To find the best in others,
To leave the world a bit better,
Whether by a healthy child, a garden patch,
Or a redeemed social condition,
To know that even one life has breathed,
Better because you have lived,
This is to have succeeded.

—Ralph Waldo Emerson

Endings are hectic and emotional. An orderly time commitment is impossible to achieve without careful planning and help from the entire staff. Culminating activities of clubs and service organizations often take place outside the school day. Many organizations have evening events in and outside of school. The principal should attend as many as possible or send an assistant principal or faculty member to represent the school.

In school, the pace is even more frenetic. The awesome process of closing activities is compounded by the need for an organized, orderly sign-out procedure. The key tasks are almost unfair to list. A new administrator can easily be overwhelmed, because each requirement is absolutely necessary. Any slow-down in efficiency in performing these end-of-year activities will have a negative ripple effect in the summer and throughout the following school year. Think of the possible ramifications of the following: retiring teachers failing to hand in classroom keys, incomplete health records for students, misplaced final examinations, teachers not leaving summer addresses, purchase orders not signed, homeroom attendance records not submitted. We could continue, but we feel the point has been made. The teacher sign-out procedures, required prior to their receiving their final salary checks, must be planned and monitored by the principal. If something goes wrong, we all know where "the buck stops."

One school lists the following items that each teacher must have initialed by a chairperson, building administrator, or the school secretary before leaving for the summer vacation: class record books, attendance registers, grade reports, failure lists (and final examinations), permanent record cards, textbook counts and locations, report cards for absentees, course outlines, and room keys. Items unique to your school can be added as necessary.

The following key tasks validate our belief that elementary school principals are master planners. An annual miracle occurs when all are accomplished in a timely fashion. We can delegate these tasks, but the final responsibility is our own. Good luck; we hope these ideas will serve as a "tickler file" to add to your own repertoire.

June's Key Tasks

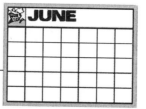

* **Summer Reading List**

One of the more exciting innovations has been the growth of summer reading programs. Once exclusively for advanced secondary school students, it is presently an elementary method to increase the joy of reading for all children in grades K-5. During May and June, teachers and librarians develop a list of books that are appropriate for each grade level. Not only are many of these books age appropriate, but they are also often tied to curriculum requirements. The selection exercise, which involves the entire staff, is educationally beneficial to all.

Some schools offer an awards program for students in September depending upon how many books are read. Parents must certify that their children did indeed read the books. Many parents have reported that they have gone to the neighborhood library throughout the summer in order to select and replenish their child's book supply. We personally observed such an awards assembly and are pleased to announce that their classmates applauded each of the children who read books and received a token of recognition for their efforts.

Personal Commentary/Notes: _____

_____

Final Report Cards *

Use the final distribution of report cards as an opportunity to give parents suggestions to help prepare their children for the coming school year. Make sure you are available for a few days immediately after report cards go home. You will be able to answer many of the questions and concerns parents may have. If not, have staff members call parents to inform them of procedures involved in signing up their student for summer school courses if needed. Recommend summer tutoring if it is indicated.

Personal Commentary/Notes: _____

_____

Review Final Grades and Retention *

The principal should prepare a comprehensive report for the superintendent on the end-of-the-year grades and the number of students who are going to be retained. This report should also serve as an opportunity to meet with department chairpersons and specific teachers to improve instructional practices and adjust the curriculum. Keep all teacher grade books on file in the event a parent makes an inquiry after your staff leaves for the summer vacation. Parents and students may want to review the grading of a particular examination or state assessment result. These, too, must be available upon request.

Personal Commentary/Notes: _____

_____

End-of-the-Year Reports *

Do not put off completing the many end-of-the-year reports required by your district and state. Double-check each report, because a small mistake may be compounded in any district or state report that is made public. You may want to list your district's requirements, such as:

1. Student attendance

2. Number retained

3. Summer school attendees

4. Teacher retirements

5. Teacher hiring

*Personal Commentary/Notes:*_____

_____

* Locker Cleanout

The final locker cleanout can also become part of the preparation process for the opening of school next year. Have each classroom teacher check each locker and report on any that need repairs or attention. This will help the custodial staff concentrate its efforts on the areas that are most critical. Cubbies in classrooms should also be emptied prior to the end of school.

*Personal Commentary/Notes:*_____

_____

* Graduation

The principal sets the tone for the moving-up exercise at rehearsal and in communications made to the parents. Some schools that have experienced over-crowding are forced to limit the number of tickets. Oversee the distribution of tickets and the production of the program. Triple-check the spelling and pronunciation of each child's name to avoid embarrassing situations. Meet with all staff serving on the graduation committee before the ceremony to discuss responsibilities and afterward to generate suggestions for improving the next year's event.

*Personal Commentary/Notes:*_____

_____

* Awards Assembly

The annual academic awards program is often a long and drawn-out affair. Work with the presenters to keep the program moving. Remind all of behavior expectations, and provide everyone with a program list of the award winners after the event is over. This should not replicate a typical high school program. Awards for improvement in academic areas, service to the community, better citizenship, and assistance with younger students should replace the traditional valedictorian selection.

*Personal Commentary/Notes:*_____

_____

Special Awards Program ✳

A society based on the recipients of the president's academic performance standards plus teacher input has proven very successful in several districts. This celebration is held in June with all elementary schools participating (as this pre-empts the obvious comparisons between schools). Individual letters of invitation are mailed home to qualifying students, plaques are ordered, a brief ceremony with a speaker is arranged, and refreshments are provided. At one school last year, over 800 parents and friends attended the celebration. At the school level, we keep a low profile of the celebration, hoping to ensure that there is not an exaggerated sense of competition or peer pressure. It is a real shared family honor that is greatly appreciated by all.

Personal Commentary/Notes: _____

_____

Summer School ✳

Provide all students and parents with an opportunity to register early for summer school. This will assist parents in planning for the summer and will give the summer school administrator an idea of the number of students attending.

Personal Commentary/Notes: _____

_____

Sign-Out ✳

The principal should publish a comprehensive end-of-the-year checklist for teachers. This should include a cover sheet with a list of materials due and a place for the appropriate staff member to initial that the item has been completed. Set a distinct time for final check-out, and be sure to work with the office staff to make this process go smoothly. (See Resource P—End-of-the-Year Sign-Out Checklist.)

Personal Commentary/Notes: _____

_____

Attend Activities ✳

Keep your calendar clear during the last few days of school to handle the last-minute issues that almost always develop. Be sure to schedule time to attend all of the closing events, and use your speaking opportunities to thank people for their contributions during the year.

Personal Commentary/Notes: _____

_____

✳ Summer Work

Send the superintendent your recommendations for summer curriculum writing and summer staffing. Provide those teachers assigned to curriculum writing with formats to use as a model. Finally, submit your vacation schedule to your immediate supervisor.

*Personal Commentary/Notes:*_____

_____

✳ Books and Equipment

Collecting books and equipment is a major undertaking. Work with the staff to create a record-keeping system that is easy to use and understand. Notify parents of any outstanding books or equipment loans as soon as possible, indicating the times and locations to return these items. This is an appropriate task for each grade-level leader.

*Personal Commentary/Notes:*_____

_____

June's Communications

✳ Board of Education Presentation

The June board of education meeting is a time of transition. The newly elected board members are preparing to take office and are anxious to learn about the schools. Use your presentation to highlight the major accomplishments of the year and to begin to identify the goals and special events coming in the next school year. You may want to invite new board members for a tour of your facility.

*Personal Commentary/Notes:*_____

_____

✳ PTA Installation Night

The annual PTA installation night is another opportunity for the principal to acknowledge the most active and supportive parents. At the same time, parents want and respect a principal who tells it like it is. Balance the positive comments with an honest assessment of the areas that the school must continue work on to improve. The elementary schools have the highest level of parent involvement in most school districts. Thank your PTA for all its efforts on behalf of the children and your staff.

Personal Commentary/Notes: _____

_____

Summer Schedule *

Communication is an important function for every principal. Continue to reach out to staff over the summer with letters and with offers of opportunities for direct contact. Let all staff members know your summer schedule, and invite them to visit at any time. A teacher visit in the summer often validates your request for staff input. The calm summer atmosphere is conducive to sharing concerns and solving problems. Conversations will not be interrupted by the bell!

Personal Commentary/Notes: _____

_____

Faculty Interviews *

Use the calm pace of the summer to meet individually with staff members. Plan for these meetings by developing a list of questions that focus on the broad issues educators should be addressing as well as handling the routine concerns and problems.

Personal Commentary/Notes: _____

_____

June's Planning

Failure Lists *

Make the reporting of failing report cards and grade retention a priority. A personal call to parents with information about options will be appreciated. No parent should be surprised by a failure if teachers have done a good job with ongoing communication and the progress report system.

Personal Commentary/Notes: _____

_____

✳ *Summer Cleaning*

Meet with the head custodian to develop a summer cleaning schedule for the building. Be sure to avoid conflicts with summer school. Check the condition of each room, and give as many areas of the school as possible a fresh coat of paint. You must establish the priorities.

*Personal Commentary/Notes:*_____

_____

✳ *Teachers' and Chairpersons' Schedules*

Keep the summer schedule of your teachers and chairpersons close at hand. They are critical in responding to the many questions that may come up over the summer. Sudden retirements, concern over a grade, and a special report requested by the superintendent are all examples of the types of issues they may help you solve.

*Personal Commentary/Notes:*_____

_____

✳ *Opening*

By now, planning should be well under way for the opening of school. Welcome-back letters, materials, and supplies should be organized and prepared. The activity calendar and a list of meetings should now be on the next year's calendar.

*Personal Commentary/Notes:*_____

_____

June's Personnel

✳ *Evaluations*

All faculty and staff evaluations should be completed by the close of school. Have your secretary keep a list of all such documents, and have her remind you of any outstanding evaluations. These should be sent to the central office prior to the annual due date.

*Personal Commentary/Notes:*_____

_____

Teaching Schedule ✳

Teachers are often anxious about their schedules for the coming year. Coordinate with other administrators and your secretary to release this information to all staff at the same time. Be sure to explain that all schedules are tentative, because some changes may be necessary over the summer. Parental notification of teacher schedules is usually withheld until the start of school. Teacher preference can be an explosive issue. We recommend that it remain a school decision, as it is one of the few areas in which we feel that flexibility leads to major problems.

Personal Commentary/Notes: _____

_____

June's Checklists

June's Key Tasks and Reminders

Major Assignments	Date Started	Date Completed	Days on Task
Issue summer reading list suggestions			
Issue final report cards			
Review final grades and retention			
Complete all state and superintendent's end-of-the-year reports			
Organize final locker cleanout			
Conduct graduation ceremony			
Organize awards assembly			
Run early registration for summer school			
Publish teacher sign-out procedures			
Attend end-of-the-year activities			

(continued)

June's Key Tasks and Reminders (continued)

Major Assignments	Date Started	Date Completed	Days on Task
Submit summer work recommendations			
Develop a list of students who have not returned books or equipment			

June's Communications Checklist

✔	Assignment
	Provide board of education with plans for the upcoming year
	Attend PTA installation night
	Notify faculty and staff of summer schedule
	Set up schedule of faculty interviews and meetings

June's Planning Checklist

✔	Assignment
	Develop deadlines for submission of grades and failure lists
	Meet with head custodian to finalize summer cleaning and painting schedule
	Review all chairpersons' schedules and vacation dates
	Develop preliminary plans for opening of school

June's Personnel Checklist

✔	Finalize
	Have secretary check that all evaluations have been completed
	Announce next year's teaching schedules

JUNE CALENDAR

MONTH: JUNE

YEAR: _____

MONDAY ___	TUESDAY ___	WEDNESDAY ___	THURSDAY ___	FRIDAY ___	SATURDAY / SUNDAY ___
MONDAY ___	TUESDAY ___	WEDNESDAY ___	THURSDAY ___	FRIDAY ___	SATURDAY / SUNDAY ___
MONDAY ___	TUESDAY ___	WEDNESDAY ___	THURSDAY ___	FRIDAY ___	SATURDAY / SUNDAY ___
MONDAY ___	TUESDAY ___	WEDNESDAY ___	THURSDAY ___	FRIDAY ___	SATURDAY / SUNDAY ___
MONDAY ___	TUESDAY ___	WEDNESDAY ___	THURSDAY ___	FRIDAY ___	SATURDAY / SUNDAY ___

Notes: _____

144

Resources

Resource A
Teacher Handbook

Absences

Should it be necessary for you to be absent from school, please do the following:

1. Call the main office immediately after 7:00 a.m.

2. Complete absence forms in duplicate; forms are available in the main office.

Academically Gifted Program

Children are chosen on a districtwide, competitive basis. All eligible district elementary school students, including those from parochial schools, are put into a pool; academic scores, teacher recommendations, and results of case conferences are all weighed before a final decision is made. The names of our third, fourth, and fifth graders in the program will be in your opening day packet. Classes will meet at the school during the following times:

Third grade: Wednesday, 9:00 to 11:00 a.m.

Fourth grade: Thursday, 9:00 to 11:00 a.m.

Fifth grade: Tuesday, 9:00 to 11:00 a.m.

Accidents

Please report any and all accidents to our school nurse immediately. After attending to the child or adult, the nurse will complete the necessary accident form.

Annual Professional Plan

In our district, we believe that education and educators must strive for professional and instructional improvement through a cycle of staff development, supervision, and evaluation, with all three phases being mutually supportive and interdependent. A mutually agreed-upon annual plan will be developed between an evaluator and staff member. The plan may include the following components: staff development, supervision, and evaluation. The staff member may enter the cycle for professional or instructional improvement at any mutually agreed-upon juncture. However, there is a more specific formula for nontenured members. Other variations and more details may be found in each staff member's personal package, titled "Staff Development, Supervision, and Evaluation Plan."

Attendance: Students

Attendance slips must be sent to the office promptly by 9:00 a.m. State law requires a note from a parent or guardian stating the reason for the student's absence. This note must accompany the child upon his or her return to school. Please be vigilant in obtaining the note. Then place the note in a large envelope clearly marked with the school year. This information will be collected at the end of the year for permanent filing. The white state attendance register cards should be completed for each student on a five-week basis. The information may be then transferred to the pink computer forms that you will receive in your mailbox. To add or delete a student, follow the instructions using the pink "add" or "delete" forms.

Attendance: Teachers

Teachers' hours Monday through Thursday are from 8:08 a.m. to 2:40 p.m. On Fridays, hours are from 7:45 a.m. to 2:40 p.m.

Because attendance information is computerized, you are required to give a reason for your absence when calling. Classroom teachers are required to be in their classrooms in time to begin classes promptly at 8:23. All teachers must sign in by 8:08 a.m. because this is the only way of verifying whether or not you are present. Should an emergency arise preventing your arrival, the principal uses the sign-in sheet to determine whether coverage is necessary for your class. This is also true for special teachers. Should a teacher arrive late, a Tardy Form must be completed. It is a legal requirement and may be used as such to verify attendance. No one is permitted to sign in for a colleague.

Block Scheduling

Grades 2, 3, 4, and 5 will be utilizing a management system for the primary purpose of

1. Eliminating as many pull-outs as possible

2. Maximizing the instruction of both the classroom teacher and the specialists

Parallel block scheduling gives teachers blocks of uninterrupted time for instruction. While one group of students remains with the classroom teacher for directed instruction, the other group of students moves out of the classroom to an extension center. Students in need of support services will go to that special service during that block of time instead of attending the extension center.

Bulletin Boards

Fire-retardant materials must be used on all hall bulletin boards. The custodians have a special spray for this purpose. We recognize that classroom bulletin boards are an integral adjunct to classroom instruction and learning. Children's work should be attractively displayed with frequent changes in order to "showcase" as many pieces of work as possible. Please utilize this important tool to reinforce your classroom teaching.

Calendar

The large calendar on the bulletin board in the main office contains important information about school events. Please consult it frequently for updating. Also, you are asked to fill in all confirmed field trips and notify the dining room personnel should your class not be eating in school. You will receive a monthly calendar of events for your planning purposes that reiterates the information on the main calendar.

Chain of Command

In the principal's absence, please see our learning specialist. Should he or she be unavailable, please check with our secretary for the name of the person who has been placed in charge.

Child Abuse or Neglect Suspicions

Any suspicious circumstances (bruises, unusual marks, extraordinary tardiness over an extended period of time, apparent hunger, etc.) must be reported to the principal for immediate follow-up. State law binds us to report any suspicious case. Of course, you are protected by anonymity in this regard. The rule is always "better safe than sorry."

Child Study Team

The Child Study Team consists of the principal, learning specialist, nurse, psychologist, resource room teacher, and invited teacher(s). The purpose of the team, which meets monthly on a Tuesday morning, is to review recommendations to the committee. The Child Study Team acts when and if the recommendation of the committee finds it necessary to recommend a formal evaluation of a student in need. Your concerns are not limited and may range from needing advice about a very bright child not working up to potential, to a less capable student about whom you would like to consult for help. Specific information will be provided at this meeting should it be necessary to proceed with a full evaluation.

Communication

Please keep the principal informed of matters that require special attention. For example, prior to sending a note home regarding lack of progress, inattentiveness, or deportment, please communicate with the principal. Frequent contact with both principal and parents is encouraged and serves to benefit the child. The lines of communication must be kept open to all involved.

Conflict Resolution

In an effort to assist children in resolving their problems in an appropriate, effective manner, a program of conflict resolution has been established. Many teachers and students have been trained as conflict managers. Teams of students help peers who are experiencing difficulties. Children are asked by an adult if they wish to take advantage of going to "mediation" about their problem. Should all parties agree, an appointment is made (always during the students' lunch hour) by one of the moderators of the program. A student team plus a trained adult will be available for a mediation session. The adult is located in reasonable proximity to the student session and is called upon in case of an urgent need that cannot be settled appropriately by the students. Each teacher will receive forms (which will remain permanently in your room) to be used for conflict resolution purposes.

Counseling

Particular situations might require the intervention of our school psychologist. Please confer with either our psychologist or the principal regarding a concern you might have in this regard. A Consultation Form will be required by you to give all the involved personnel some pertinent background information. Our school psychologist will arrange for counseling sessions in cases that require his or her intervention.

Custodian

Should anyone need a custodian, please notify the main office, where custodial contact will be made for you. Please do not send children to deliver messages for this purposes. In an emergency, use your classroom intercom. (See details under "Intercom" for easy use of this tool.)

Detaining a Student

Should you find it necessary to detain a child after school hours, 24-hour notice to parents is an absolute requirement. Please adhere to this regulation, because parents have the right to know in advance so that they will be able to change or postpone a prearranged appointment such as a dental or doctor's visit.

Dining Room

Proper dining room behavior is expected of each child. Teachers supervising must ensure that children are sitting while eating and that passes are issued for bathroom or computer room use. Teachers picking up children should wait at the dining room door for the lunch supervisor to dismiss classes. Please arrive two to three minutes early, as it is necessary to allow incoming students the opportunity to proceed without a traffic jam.

Directors

Fortunately, we have on staff in our district a K-12 director for each of the curriculum areas. These knowledgeable men and women are available to you and can be an invaluable resource in your work. Speak with the principal for guidance and direction in this matter, because appointments may be arranged for you with the appropriate director should you need advice or help.

Discipline With Dignity

1. Routine difficulties should be handled by the classroom or special teacher.

2. Mediation with a trained student (and with a trained teacher within reasonable proximity) is a fair option.

3. Repeated instances of misbehavior should be referred to the principal for assistance and strategy. However, should a situation arise that presents an unsafe condition for a student or those around him or her, it is absolutely imperative that you use the intercom to contact the office for immediate help. Do not leave your room; help will arrive immediately. In the meantime, please avoid using physical contact if at all possible. Instead, techniques such as trying to isolate the child, trying to reason with him or her, or any other nonconfrontational approach is advisable.

4. Always notify the principal should incidents of harassment or racial slurs be committed.

5. Students may not be sent to another classroom for disciplinary reasons.

Dismissal

The time for dismissal is 2:30 p.m. for bus students to assemble, 2:35 p.m. for all other students, and 2:40 p.m. for teachers.

In order to maintain an orderly and safe dismissal, please observe the following:

1. Escort all children to their appropriate dismissal door.

2. Grades 2 and 3 are dismissed from the main lobby.

3. Grades 4 and 5 are dismissed from the northwest door. It is very important that teachers station themselves in the halls so that children don't run and become subject to injury.

4. Bus children are dismissed from the Central Road door.

5. Grade 1 will be dismissed from the Side Road exit door.

Drills

There are three basic drills with which you must be familiar:

Emergency Drill. When the air raid alarm (a loud foghorn-type alarm) sounds, students will proceed into the halls and will sit along the walls, away from windows and doors, and cradle their heads between their arms until the "all clear" is sounded. This type of drill is used in such cases as severe hurricane and so forth.

Fire Drill. When the fire alarm rings, immediately proceed to leave the building. Doors should be closed as the last student leaves each room. Classes should be taken to their assigned location, a safe distance from the building. Each teacher is responsible for ensuring that the "Exit Directions," which have been provided for each classroom, are posted near the door. Silence is necessary. Teachers must take class registers with them when they exit the building.

Class registers or attendance cards must be placed in the appropriate receptacle (affixed to the teacher's desk) for easy access of records and for quick access when a substitute teacher is in the room.

Remember: Expect the unexpected—for example, a doorway may be blocked, or a drill may take place during lunch (see procedure below). Remember that you need to think quickly and reroute your children should this occur. Once outdoors, immediately check that each child is accounted for. Specialists, please be sure that you escort your children to their homeroom location.

Go-Home Drill. In an extreme emergency, children either will be sent home or will be transported to the middle school for safety. You will be given advance notice of this drill. However, in the event of this type of emergency, you must be prepared in the following manner:

1. Take your class register with you wherever you are told to go.

2. Listen for emergency directives that will come over the public address system.

3. Should electricity be shut down, the principal or his or her designees will issue verbal directions.

Should a drill occur during a lunch hour, each of the dining room moderators (the teacher-in-charge and a teacher aide) will have a complete set of class lists.

1. If you are in the building during the drill, please assist by going directly to your regular spot outdoors.

2. The teacher-in-charge or the teacher aide will have your class list if you need it.

3. The children who are eating in the dining room will meet their teacher at their regular outdoor spot. Those children who are playing outdoors will line up at the fence with their respective classes.

Sheltering in the Event of an Emergency. In the event of an emergency when it is safe to remain in the school rather than to evacuate, all students and staff will be sheltered in the gymnasium or the auditorium. There is a "coverage for emergency drills" list furnished for your convenience. Please make sure that this list is stapled in your plan book for easy reference.

Early Arrival of Students

Students who arrive early in fair weather will use the outdoor facilities. Students who arrive early in inclement weather will be permitted to assemble in the hall outside the principal's office, providing the principal has arrived. Students' families should be discouraged from sending children to school before 8:00 a.m., because supervision is not provided prior to that hour.

English as a Second Language

The English as a Second Language (ESL) program is designed primarily as a pull-out program whose goal is to mainstream children as soon as language proficiency is attained. There are three full-time teachers assigned to the position to assist children and classroom teachers in every way possible. In addition to their teaching assignment, teachers will translate report card comments into either Spanish or Portuguese. Please submit your comments to the teachers as early as possible. Also, when you are conducting parent-teacher conferences with parents whose native language is either Portuguese or Spanish, ESL teachers will be made available.

Faculty Meetings

1. Meetings are usually held on the second Thursday of each month at 2:40 p.m. sharp and last 45 minutes. Matters of concern or interest to all faculty members are the major emphasis of the meetings. In addition, the superintendent has the contractual ability to call 10 additional meetings per year should the need arise.

2. Staff development meetings: According to contract, one 25-minute meeting will be conducted weekly at the elementary level. Our school's meetings will take place every Friday morning at 7:45 a.m. Everyone is expected to be on time, because important professional concepts to enrich our bank of knowledge will be discussed and developed.

Field Trips

1. Decide on one or two appropriate trips per year, usually discussed as a grade-level team.

2. Call the Transportation Office regarding bus availability for the particular date you have selected.

3. Fill out the appropriate form in quadruplicate. You'll find copies in the main office for your convenience.

4. Once confirmed, please make a note on the main school calendar located in the main office.

5. All money collected must be given to our secretary for safekeeping. Money may not be kept in the classroom.

6. Please collect monies well in advance of the trip so that our secretary will have adequate time to write out a check for the total cost of the trip.

Fire Codes

No desks, chairs, or any other obstructions are allowed in any hall. There is to be no obstruction on a windowsill or in front of the window marked "Fire Escape." Teachers must carry their attendance books out with them during a fire drill.

Homework

Our board of education has established regulations for homework. Strict adherence to the regulations is expected of all. Please ensure that this worthy activity is valuable. Creativity is certainly appreciated. Also appreciated is variety. As you know, many parents look to homework as one more indicator of what's happening in the classroom. It becomes an excellent monitoring tool for parents who wish to be continually involved in their child's schoolwork.

Homework Policy

As defined by the regulations of the board of education,

Homework is studying at home and is ordinarily an extension of classroom instruction.

The purpose of homework is the improvement of the learning process by reinforcing newly acquired skills, by engaging in preparatory activities such as in reading for background, and by extending and applying classroom learning for developing new and deeper understanding.

Homework should be assigned regularly to all pupils and should progressively increase in amount from the primary grades through the high school.

Teachers should ensure that assignments are made that are necessary and useful, appropriate to the ability and maturity level of students, well explained and motivating, and clearly understood by students and, where appropriate, by parents. Guidelines should be provided regarding how the homework assignment might be approached; in noting that any assignment that is worth making is worth evaluation, teachers should monitor homework carefully and provide pupils the feedback needed to enhance learning.

Principals should take steps to prepare and communicate procedures for homework and to coordinate homework assignments so that pupils are not, for example, overloaded when they have long and difficult assignments one night and have little or no homework the next, or when they return from an extended absence during which an overburdening amount of homework has accumulated.

Parents should be aware that homework assignments ordinarily indicate what pupils have been doing in school and should provide encouragement, which strengthens the link between home and school.

Homework Suggested Time Limits for Elementary School Students

Pre-K and Kindergarten: Homework is not assigned on a regular basis. Children assume the responsibility for bringing in materials. Work is assigned according to individual growth needs.

Grades 1 and 2:   Homework should be 5-10 minutes usually four times per week.

Grade 3:   Homework should be 15-20 minutes usually four times per week.

Grade 4:   Homework should be 30-40 minutes usually four times per week.

Grade 5:   Homework should be 30-45 minutes usually four times per week.

Honors Society

Children in Grades 2 through 5 are eligible to participate in the Elementary Academic Celebration based on the following criteria. First, they must achieve the President's Criteria for Academic Fitness. Then, you will be asked to decide whether each child qualifies based on a consideration of (a) academic excellence and success in class; and (b) activities in which a student demonstrates high motivation, initiative, integrity, intellectual depth, leadership qualities, or exceptional judgment.

Hospitality

The Hospitality Committee asks for an annual contribution for special occasions and parties. Individual collections are made for retirements. You are asked to keep chairpersons informed should you hear of an engagement, wedding, illness, death, or any other cause that should come to the attention of our staff. The committee will then appropriately acknowledge the occasion.

Hours

Children: 8:23 a.m. to 2:35 p.m.

Teachers Monday through Thursday: 8:08 a.m. to 2:40 p.m.

Teachers Fridays: 7:45 a.m. to 2:40 p.m.

Classroom teachers are required to be in their classrooms at a time that will comfortably allow them to begin classes promptly at 8:23 a.m.

Inclement Weather

In inclement weather, children will assemble in the gymnasium during their regularly scheduled outdoor recess time. They may be asked to bring games from home or classroom. Classroom teachers might want to provide activities for the students during this time. Teachers and aides usually assigned to outdoor recess supervise children in the gym.

For morning assembly during inclement weather,

* Pre-K will assemble in their room.

* Kindergarten will assemble in their assigned hallway.

* Grades 1, 2, and 3 will assemble in the main lobby.

* Grades 4 and 5 will assemble in the fifth-grade hallway.

Intercom

The intercom in each room is provided for your convenience and safety. Should you need to contact the main office, simply turn the switch to the On position, then announce your name and room number, and you will receive a response. Therefore, there is no need to leave your class unattended in case of emergency. As a matter of fact, you may not leave your class unattended ever!

Internet Usage

To allow our students and staff to be prepared for the 21st century, we are committed to the teaching of the most current skills to access information. We will be instructing our students about the Internet so they will be able to access information using online research. Ideally, they will find the Internet a powerful means of providing access to worldwide current events and many other useful resource skills. However, there are concerns about the user's access to inappropriate materials. In an attempt to prevent such materials from being accessed, the following precautions have been taken:

Students must be supervised at all times when they use the Internet.

All computers with Internet capability will have a filter with the purpose of blocking access to inappropriate sites.

All students and parents are required to sign an Internet Use Agreement before students are allowed to use the Internet.

Users breaking the rules of the contract may have their privileges revoked.

Violation of the agreement may also result in disciplinary and/or appropriate legal action.

Keys

Classroom keys are distributed on the first day of school and are to be returned to the main office on the last day of school.

Lateness

Students who arrive after 8:23 a.m. must report to the office before reporting to class. This will eliminate the need to call home to verify a perceived absence and thus will avoid much confusion.

Learning Fair

This is an annual event in which teachers participate by displaying all children's works. Classroom teachers will be provided time during the school day to set up a display in the gym. The fair is held on the budget vote night and has a threefold purpose:

1. To provide the entire community with an opportunity to see firsthand their children's work at the elementary level

2. To inspire a larger number of people to come out to vote

3. To exhibit exemplary models of work that set a high standard for all

Learning Specialist

The learning specialist administers academic screening to

1. New entrants to our school

2. Suspected learning-disabled students

3. Retention candidates

4. Pre-K registrants

5. Students who are recommended for remediation

The learning specialist will coordinate the writing and reading programs for the building and serve as the resource person for curriculum. Demonstration lessons will also be provided by the learning specialist, especially in the area of creative writing or for integrating language arts with content areas. Please see the learning specialist for arrangements.

Lesson Plans

According to district policy, lesson plans must contain goals, objectives, evaluation, and homework assignments. Please circle the word *homework* in red so that it is obvious. For plan book review in Grades 1 through 5, select either Monday or Tuesday weekly. For Kindergarten and specials, review shall be the first Monday of each month. Submit plan books before 8:30 a.m. Substitute plans should be completed monthly and written clearly in back of the plan book.

Local Newspaper

One way to keep our citizens informed of school happenings is for each teacher to submit one article per year for publication. Please make sure that the "story" is an interesting one; it may be accompanied by a photo. All classroom teachers and specials need to participate in this community service function. A camera and film will be provided for your convenience.

Locks

There should be at least one secured closet or drawer in each classroom. Should that not be the case, please notify our head custodian immediately. Also, all classrooms must be locked during the lunch hour and when you leave the room during a professional planning period. This practice will eliminate the temptation for someone to enter the room and remove something from it.

Lunch Count

An accurate count of lunches should be made by 9:00 a.m. and sent to the dining room. Please indicate the specific lunches on the ticket, especially if there are two lunches offered on the menu for the day. Teachers' lunches are available for you and should be indicated on the lunch form if you wish to order. Reminder: Should your class be on a field trip and not eating in the dining room, please notify the cafeteria personnel one week in advance.

Medication

Only the nurse may administer medication from a properly labeled jar or bottle. Should students or parents advise you of the need to take medication of any kind, please refer them to the nurse immediately. No medicine may be given without a physician's note submitted to the nurse. This is also the case with simple aspirin or cough medicine. Please be very observant about this, as it can present far-reaching negative ramifications.

Meet Your Teacher Night

Each year, we hold an evening meeting for parents. This year, Monday, September 18, is the date of our Meet Your Teacher Night. The purpose of the evening is to meet and greet your parents and to provide an opportunity for each of you to introduce yourselves early in the year. It is not a time for individual conferences; however, it is a time to schedule them. Please supply a sign-up sheet for parents so that they may choose a convenient time during the regularly scheduled parent-teacher conference times coming up soon.

Here are some suggestions you might wish to consider:

*   Have an outline written on the chalkboard so that you will address all the issues you intend to address.

*   Talk about reading, its importance, and the philosophy of our reading program.

*   Homework expectations: How much parental help do you expect? Do you expect homework to be signed? What are the procedures when homework is not completed?

*   Introduce class parents or just name them.

*   Suggest some proper study techniques.

*   Make sure that each parent receives a letter outlining most of these features. The letter should be uniform throughout the grade.

The schedule for the evening should include a very brief greeting and introduction. There will be four 20-minute sessions (so that parents with more than one child may have the opportunity to meet each teacher) in each classroom. Special teachers, please be available in your respective rooms.

Mission Statement and Teachers' Beliefs

Mission statements are developed by a team of teachers in our school.

"Mission Possible" seeks to develop a systematic planning process and to promote optimal growth possibilities for each of our children.

Teachers' beliefs include

*   Individual students' needs

*   Class needs

*   Teacher/child comfort

*   Self-esteem

*   Parental responsibility

*   Tolerance

To accomplish our mission, a group of teacher volunteers developed a schoolwide program called S.T.A.R.S. The acronym stands for these key concepts that we believe in and attempt to foster throughout our school: "Show sensitivity," "Try your best," "Accept others," "Respect yourself and others," and "Show responsibility."

All members of our school are responsible for fulfilling each of the S.T.A.R.S.' ethical codes.

Annual schoolwide assemblies and other motivational activities will take place throughout the year to reinforce each of these concepts.

Money

Please do not keep any money in your classroom. The main office has a safe for this purpose. Any amount of money, large or small, provides an attraction, so please be responsible in this regard.

Monthly Grade-Level Parent Communication

To accommodate parents' requests emanating from the site-based management team, each grade level is asked to send home a monthly briefing of anticipated areas that will be addressed during the coming month. This is not a newsletter of past occurrences, but rather an indication of events to come. Our purpose in this regard is simple—to provide parents with an understanding of what will be occurring in school on a monthly basis to allow them perhaps to plan family outings, trips, or discussions that will enrich the school's curriculum.

Music

We are fortunate to be able to offer both choral and instrumental music to our children. Fourth and fifth graders who wish to sing in the chorus will be invited by their teacher to sign up in early fall. There are instrumental music lessons that enable fourth and fifth graders (and some selected third graders) to participate in our band or orchestra; students will be notified by our music teachers of the schedule of lessons and practices. Each of us can help to enrich this marvelous opportunity by encouraging children to participate and to be responsible upon joining. They should recognize that it is, indeed, a privilege to be able to partake of the performing arts and that they will serve as role models to the younger members of our school community.

Orderly Conduct

Since orderly conduct is expected of each student, please use all positive measures to ensure that students understand what is meant by the term *orderly conduct*. Consistency in this regard is the major emphasis and will produce the most effective results. For example, children walking in the halls are strongly encouraged to speak very softly. Teachers must emphasize respect for those people in classrooms. Therefore, only talking in low tones is permitted. Running in the halls is never permitted and must be monitored by each adult in the building. Safety must be uppermost in everyone's actions. When children use the bathrooms or other facilities, it is imperative that they be continually instructed in respecting school property.

Parent-Teacher Association (PTA)

The PTA meets monthly on the first Monday in the school dining room at 7:30 p.m. Faculty representatives act as liaisons between the PTA and teachers. You are always cordially invited to attend these meetings. As a matter of fact, parents truly enjoy the opportunity to meet and chat on an informal basis about school-related programs, not necessarily about individual children.

Parent-Teacher Conferences

A Conference Form, which can be found in the main office, must be completed for each conference that you hold with a parent or parents. At the completion of the conference, the signed white form is given to the parent, and the yellow form is filed in the student's cumulative folder. At least one conference with each child's parent(s) is required per year. However, for students who need closer supervision, regular conferencing with parents is required and expected. Of course, the principal must be kept apprised of such occurrences. Remember, a conference form must be completed for each conference. Important telephone conferences may also be documented in written form and should be sent home for the parent's signature and then filed. This will serve to keep accurate accounts and documentation of events that are worthy of note. Suggestions for conducting a successful parent-teacher conference will be discussed at length prior to the first scheduled conference. Teachers will be asked to share success stories, because this will be a valuable experience for all. Often, one suggestion makes a world of difference in meeting with parents.

Parking

Our secretary will designate a parking space for you.

Passes

It is necessary to issue a pass to students who will leave the dining room to use the computer lab during lunch. Passes are also required to enter the building from the playground at lunchtime. If you plan to meet with a student before school, please give him or her a pass the previous day so that he or she may enter the building without being questioned.

Petty Cash

Although small amounts of money are available for emergency needs, you must consult with our school secretary for confirmation prior to spending your own money should a need arise.

Quiet Zone

This is an area set aside in the courtyard with tables and benches donated by the PTA where children may elect to sit and talk or play board games during their lunch recess. No active games are permitted in this area; however, it is a splendid spot for children who wish or need to take advantage of the area. The area is not to be used for homework makeup or for punishment assignments. Please use other alternatives.

Reading Program

For the sake of consistency between and among the four elementary schools, our school district has adopted a reading program. The program is outlined for parents in their "Elementary School Parent Guide Book." It consists of the following elements: Read To, Shared Reading, Guided Reading, and Guided Writing. Inservice and training have been and will continue to be provided to teachers to ensure the proper implementation of the philosophy and materials and the continuous progress of students. Updating will be given to you regularly by the principal or the coordinator of the program.

Records

Please check the "Students With Health Conditions List" provided by our school nurse. Also, inform the nurse of any condition about which you may be aware that is not listed.

Review cumulative folders. There are two schools of thought on this issue: "I don't want to be predisposed" or "I want to know my children before meeting them." However, with the myriad of issues facing us these days, the latter approach must take precedence, because a well-informed educator is better able to serve his or her students. In addition, there are pieces of information on some children that you absolutely must know. For example, there may be a case of divorced or separated parents in which one parent may have full custody and release to the other is not permitted; for another example, certain children are absolutely forbidden to be released to a particular person or persons, and so forth.

Report Cards

Each teacher is required to make comments on each child's progress. When writing comments, please be specific in what it is you are saying. Words such as *good, should do better,* and *daydreams* are not helpful to either parents or future teachers. Should you need assistance in phrasing a remark, do not hesitate to ask an experienced colleague or the principal. If possible, typing provides an excellent medium for ensuring that your comments will be clear on the final copy. Otherwise, a heavy hand and neatness are a must! Be very conscious of your handwriting. It is imperative that the presentation paints a positive picture of you! Always check the report card for proper symbol usage and correct spelling. Pluses and minuses are not permitted.

Resource Room

The primary responsibility of the resource room teacher is to address learning disabilities of students who have been approved by the Committee on Special Education. The resource room teacher and classroom teacher will arrange the most suitable schedule for each student. These arrangements will be compatible with the parallel block scheduling.

Retention

Discussion of candidates should be held with the principal. Then, the name(s) of student(s) for possible retention should be submitted at the end of the second marking period with an appropriate remark on the report card. Referral forms will be forwarded to you for completion to provide a more comprehensive student profile. The child or children will then be tested by the learning specialist and the psychologist. The retention team, including you, the teacher, and any other support teacher who services the child or children, will meet. A letter to the parents or guardians notifying them of the retention possibility is sent from the principal's office. Final determination is made by the principal in May.

Review of Test Results

If a parent makes a request to review a child's standardized test results, please direct that parent to the principal for an appointment should you not feel comfortable interpreting the records.

Visitor's Rose

Whenever a visitor comes to our school, he or she is required to stop at the main office to receive a red rose. That rose becomes evidence to you that the person has been approved to be in the building and that his or her presence is welcomed. Please feel free to stop any adult (familiar or unfamiliar) who does not have a rose and ask that person to please go to the main office to pick one up. Security is vital, and the rose (rather than a "visitor's badge") is a less obtrusive sign of proper welcoming. Of course, it goes without saying that if you are met with an unpleasant or confrontational attitude, you should use your intercom to notify the main office immediately. To further ensure safety, only one door located by the main office is open during the day. When a person enters, a bell sounds in the main office and a video camera is activated to allow for visual identification of the individual.

Rules of Conduct

Please help make students aware of the following:

Fighting (even "play fighting") is not ever allowed.

Gum chewing is not allowed anywhere in the building.

Running in school is not permitted.

A pass is required of all students who have permission to use the computer lab.

Children using bathrooms during the lunch hour will be required to carry a pass.

Touching, kicking, or making snowballs is absolutely prohibited for safety's sake.

Please review these few rules frequently, and encourage children to observe them both for their sakes and for the sake of their schoolmates.

Safety Patrol

Fifth-grade students who are on the safety patrol display responsibility and good citizenship in the following manner: They are expected to be on post at 8:00 a.m. to see that children do not enter the school early (unless with a pass). They are expected to be on post at 2:35 p.m. to assist teachers or aides in walking children to the bus and to provide good models for younger children. They give warnings to children about unsafe activities and report children to our safety patrol monitor should the children not observe the safety patrol student's advice. They remind, encourage, and model excellent safety rules for their fellow students.

Schedules

You will be provided with a copy of your weekly schedule of specials. This period shall be used by you as a professional preparation time. Although every effort will be made to preserve the one preparation time per day, extenuating circumstances may occasionally arise that require your cooperation and understanding and that may cause the elimination of your preparation time. Please do not alter your schedule in any way unless you first consult with the principal. Please do not leave the building during your prep time without informing the principal or the secretary of the main office. This is a safety precaution for both you and your students. For example, should an unanticipated incident occur to prevent you from returning to school in time for your next class, it is urgent that coverage be provided for you and for your students. If there is a special program being held during your prep time, then the special teacher is responsible for accompanying and supervising your class at that time.

Science Resource Teacher

Our science resource teacher (SRT) will assist you with science materials, supplies, suggestions, or information. Do, however, give her two to three days lead time to prepare and gather your materials. Also, should you have any suggestions for improvement of curriculum, please notify our SRT, who will convey the information to our director of science.

Secretary

The secretary of our main office is an invaluable source of information. Please feel free to check with the secretary should you have any procedural questions or should you be in need of forms such as insurance, report cards, supplies, and so forth.

Shared-Decision-Making/Site-Based Team

There are 11 members on our school's site-based team: 4 teachers, 4 parents, 1 administrator with districtwide responsibility, the principal, and 1 community member. The team will meet monthly, with notices of meetings posted for convenience on the bulletin board outside the main office. The site-based team is defined as "an organizational strategy for the participation of parents, community representatives, teachers, and other members of the school staff and administration (including students); it helps to decentralize authority and the decision-making process."

The plan for our school district has been developed by a committee of teachers, parents, and administrators with the approval of the board of education in compliance with the state's educational commissioner. The plan includes seven parts: the educational issues that will be subject to shared decision making, the manner and extent of involvement of all parties, the means for assessing improved student performance, the ways in which the building committees will be accountable for their decisions, a dispute resolution process, the manner in which existing state and federal regulations for parent involvement will be coordinated in the plan, and training in the shared-decision-making process.

Smoking

Smoking is prohibited everywhere in the building.

Speech Services

Our speech pathologist evaluates students who have been referred for speech and/or language services. This person provides instruction in articulation and language development in individual or small-group settings. Should you have a question about a perceived need, please submit your concern to the speech pathologist.

Student Council

Four executive officers elected from the fifth-grade student body, along with third- and fourth-grade class representatives, led by their moderator, compose the Student Council. The goal is to instill a love and understanding of the value of community service and leadership. Many activities are performed during the year to accomplish this goal.

A teacher moderator conducts elections, held twice a year, for our Student Council. Elected members meet regularly to discuss items pertaining to improving school conditions and enhancing student involvement in school affairs. Fifth-grade students are elected to the executive board, which consists of a president, vice president, secretary, and treasurer. In addition, each fifth-grade class elects two representatives. Two fourth graders from each class serve as class representatives as well. Third graders join the ranks of class representatives at the midyear election. Student Council is an exciting activity that teaches children about community involvement, leadership, responsibility, and volunteerism. We encourage young students to take leadership roles and to start young!

Supervision of Children

Never leave a class unsupervised. In the case of an emergency, use the intercom to secure assistance. An accident only takes a few seconds, and you, the principal, and the school may be held liable. Always lock your classroom doors when the class is out of the room for such activities as specials instruction, lunch, and so forth. Please walk children to main lobby or exit doors for dismissal. This will help to avoid accidents and disruptive behavior.

Supplies

Supplies such as chalk, pens, paper, and so forth should be requested from the main office. Please submit your request in writing and place it in the appropriate mailbox located in the main office. Our secretary will make every effort to fill your request as soon as possible. Please do not send children to the secretary during the day, because it will not be possible to accommodate your request at that time.

Teacher Aides

You should contact the secretary of the main office whenever you need time for your aide to accompany your class on a field trip or if you need to change your teacher aide's time in any way.

TEAMS (Together we Evaluate, Assess, Modify, Support)

TEAMS is a concept developed to help all teachers who desire consultation or help in addressing concerns about a student or students. You, the teacher, will be invited to a meeting after having completed the necessary paperwork needed to start the process. The focuses of the meeting will be

To review the child's strengths

To identify one concern that is impeding learning

To generate suggestions from the members with you on how to address the concern

To choose three suggestions (different from the ones you perhaps already tried) to facilitate learning

Here's how we plan to conduct the meeting:

In the first five minutes, the teacher will identify the student's strengths to set a positive tone and to establish a foundation upon which to build. Then the teacher will identify and explain the difficulty that the student is having and the steps that have already been taken to address the problem. In the next five minutes, the team will ask any questions for clarification of the difficulty or the procedures already followed. In the next ten minutes, the team (including you, of course) will brainstorm as they look for practical suggestions to address the problem at hand. In the next five minutes, the presenting teacher will select strategies that seem most promising or appropriate to address the problem. In the final five minutes, an implementation plan will be established and recorded. Also, a timeline will be set up to evaluate progress.

Telephone

There are two telephones in the main office that may be used by teachers to conduct school business. For your personal convenience, there is a pay phone outside the main office. Also, although cellular phones are quite a convenience, please do not make use of your private phone during school hours. Emergency or important calls should be directed to the office, and you will be notified immediately of the call if so requested by the caller.

Translations

Letters or report cards that need translation should be given to a member of our ESL staff. These competent people need at least two days' advance notice to complete the task, especially during busy times of the year such as report card time. They are also available for parent-teacher conferences. Again, adequate lead time is requested.

Weekly Bulletin

A bulletin containing items of interest, important happenings, professional literature, and so forth will be distributed on Friday afternoons in your mailbox. Should you wish to contribute an article, please feel free to do so. All you need to do is submit your contribution to our secretary or the principal so that it may be included in the bulletin. Also, should you hear of a special occurrence, the awarding of a particular honor, or another special event, please inform the principal or office staff so that this information can be included for all to read.

Duplicating Material

Requests for copying must be put in the appropriate mailbox located in the main office. Please allow at least two full days for service. Also, no more than five pieces of duplicating material per week may be given to the person in charge of xeroxing. In fairness to all, this rule must be followed, and it will be strictly monitored. Under extraordinary conditions, the person in charge of xeroxing will check with the principal for clearance. Your understanding in this matter is greatly appreciated.

Resource B
How to Build a Mission Statement

Many schools are like rudderless ships, riding the waves of fad and reform from one end of the education spectrum to the other. Innovation and change in schools frequently mirror innovation and change in society as a whole; however, because of the diversity of public opinion and expectations regarding the role of the schools, individuals and groups in society may not agree about the role of schools, regardless of the current trends and fads.

These disagreements may be based on cognitive versus affective, individual versus societal, vocational versus academic, and religious versus secular ideas.

As these different emphases pull against one another, the rudder of the school turns from side to side in a futile effort to accommodate both.

When faced with this situation, an effective school demonstrates the characteristics of a high-performance organization with a commonly held sense of mission as a foundation, able to steer its own course through the maze of societal hopes and expectations.

Effective schools confront conflicting societal expectations with a firm sense of where they are headed. Although not discounting the wishes of parents and other community groups, such schools clearly state their priorities from the outset.

A written mission statement is a highly visible feature of effective schools. In addition to stating the school's priorities, it reflects the commitment of the administration and staff to the school's mission.

The Role of the Principal

Staff members will probably not feel a common sense of mission unless the principal has taken an active role in formulating and articulating that mission. This role may include direct involvement in the formulation of the statement, the writing of the statement, or at least close contact with the committee charged with writing the statement.

Leaders of effective schools operate with a dual vision that includes both where they see the school now and what they see it becoming in the future. Whatever their leadership style, these schools concentrate on those activities that will close the gap between the two visions.

The mission statement is an important vehicle whereby the principal may communicate this dual vision to staff, students, and the community and may give purpose to the daily activities of the school. Too often, principals see their role as managing what is, rather than leading toward what could be. Such administrators may relate well to staff members and students and may effectively maintain the daily routine, but they are not leaders whose actions will motivate staff and students toward significant school improvement.

Administrators must not be afraid that by expressing their conceptions of a good school and its mission they will "stir up trouble." They can provide valuable, useful guidance. Above all else, leaders of high-performing systems carry out the mission of their organizations.

Developing a Mission Statement

Developing a mission statement and articulating a sense of mission requires effort, perseverance, communication, human relations skills, a sense of vision, and a willingness to publicly affirm one's beliefs. When developing a mission statement, principals should consider the following:

* The mission statement must be clearly articulated. Some administrators communicate a sense of mission by example (i.e., symbolic actions, time allocations, etc.), others by persuasion.

* The committee charged with writing the mission statement should include volunteers representing all the different subgroups within the staff and community; race, sex, and age equity are vital.

* Academic, vocational, and special education teachers should be represented, as well as parents and retired persons from the community.

* In spite of the heterogeneous makeup of the group, the committee members should share a commitment to base the mission statement on group consensus; the statement should reflect the beliefs upon which everyone agrees.

* As a starting place, the committee might solicit staff and community members' views about their philosophy of education, child growth and development, and the roles of teachers and parents in this process. A brief questionnaire might accomplish this first step.

* Once committee members begin drafting the mission statement, frequent communication among committee members, staff members, and community members is important.

* Representatives from these groups should have the opportunity to review and edit successive drafts of the statement. The principal should play an important role as a communications liaison.

* The document should be written in short, logically connected statements that clearly reflect specific goals. During the revision process, superfluous statements will be eliminated so that the final drafted form will not exceed one page.

* When completed, the mission statement should be posted throughout the school—in the main office, in hallways, and in each classroom.

* Copies can also be displayed in local community centers and businesses, anywhere that people connected with the school gather. A copy should also be sent to every parent.

* The mission statement should serve as a guide in orientation sessions for new staff members, students, parents, and school visitors. Principals should rely on the statement to explain the rationale for any school policy or practice.

* The administration and staff should consciously strive, through word and action, to symbolize their commitment to the mission statement.

* At some point, students, especially those at the secondary level, should be encouraged to develop their own mission statement. Many of the suggestions in this list would apply to a student mission statement.

* Program, policy, and procedural changes within the school should take place with the mission statement in mind. It should serve as the rationale for change.

* Do not allow the mission statement to become a philosophical straitjacket; avoid "carving the statement into stone." The committee members should periodically review the statement for possible revisions.

* High-performing, instructionally effective schools are characterized by a consensus regarding the school's basic goals.

* That such schools are able to remain on course while besieged by the demands and expectations of society is due, in part, to the fact that they know where they are headed.

Resource C
Summer Letters to Parents

Sample Parent Letter 1

Dear Parents/Guardians,

When I asked our secretary how she enjoyed her summer vacation, her reply was, "Oh yes. It was a lovely long weekend!" I don't know about you, but I share her sentiments exactly. So, here we are on the verge of a most exciting, productive, and fulfilling new year. Welcome back, one and all.

I thought you would enjoy a few simple ideas that might help you and your family gear up for a great school year (they were taken from "Parents Make a Difference!" magazine):

Make a plan for after-school activities.

Schedule adequate time for homework, play, clubs, sports, and practice.

Scale back TV time.

Establish bedtimes for school nights.

Collect important phone numbers. Update doctor, work, and other listings for the school office, after-school programs, and one or two neighbors.

Create a car pool, if possible. Compare schedules with friends, and determine which parents can drive kids when you cannot drive.

Have a backup plan. Find another parent who will exchange school pickup favors in case you get ill or delayed.

Spruce up a study space for your child(ren). Include pens, pencils, dictionary, and other needed supplies.

Get children in the habit of getting ready the night before school. Set out clothes, pack lunch, and put the backpack by the front door.

I trust these few hints will help, and I hope this will be one of the best years ever! You can depend on us to do all that we can to be cooperative, helpful, and inspiring.

Sincerely,

Your Elementary School Principal

Sample Parent Letter 2

Dear Parents/Guardians,

Prior to the beginning of a new school year, parents often ask for advice in helping their children get off to a good start in school. Surveys show that an overwhelming number of students feel that their teachers do a great job teaching and that schools do a good job teaching subject matter. However, we all know that schools can't do it all. Parents can play a vital role in helping youngsters develop strong study skills.

The following ideas come from several articles that I believe provide some useful suggestions:

Help children use a planning calendar and notebook to keep track of weekly, monthly, or large projects.

Encourage children to break down large, complex tasks into manageable pieces.

Encourage children to complete homework tasks in some order of priority. (Sometimes, it's best to do the least favorite task first.)

Don't be too concerned if your child's notes look sloppy or a bit disorganized. Active minds organize things in ways that work best for them. We've learned this from research dealing with learning styles.

Encourage young readers to use all the clues available to them while reading, such as headlines, pictures, captions, charts, tables, and graphs.

A discussion with children after reading a book or article helps with comprehension. Ask your children to tell you what the story was about, why it interested them or why not, and perhaps how it might relate to their own lives.

Should you wish to have more in-depth information, always feel free to talk to your child's teacher. He or she can provide a clearer picture of your child's learning style, strengths, and weaknesses. Also, remember, if I can be of help in this or any other matter, please feel free to call me.

With best personal regards,

Your Elementary School Principal

Resource D
Meet Your Teacher Night—
Suggestions for Teachers

1. On the chalkboard, place an outline of pertinent points to be discussed. This will provide for good time management and keep everyone on target.

2. Provide parent-teacher conference sign-up sheets in your room in order to elicit the most convenient time to meet during the scheduled parent-teacher conference days or evening. Confirmation forms may be obtained in the main office once the final determination has been made.

3. A packet of information has been provided for distribution to each parent. It contains a copy of the Parent Guidebook, Emergency Telephone Numbers Form, Emergency Go-Home Drill letter, and so forth. Should a parent not attend the meeting, please be sure that the packet is sent home with the student.

4. Children might like to write a note to parents and leave it on the desk for an answer.

5. Our PTA suggests that an invitation to join their association be extended on the chalkboard. They would also ask that you mention that they will host only four class parties per year (Halloween, Winter, Spring, End-of-the-Year).

Remember, a visually attractive room creates excellent public relations. This is especially true when children's work is displayed. Good luck and enjoy the night.

Resource E
Weekly Memo to Staff

Memorandum

To: All Staff
From: Your Principal
Re: Weekly Memo

Our school celebrated American Education Week in the following ways:

*   We held a Book Fair in which hundreds of families participated.

*   Hundreds of books were donated to our school library as a result of the book sales.

*   We held two opportunities for parents to visit our school. Over 200 parents visited and were treated to many wonderful activities.

*   A Book and Author Tea featuring a famous children's author was held on Friday evening. She was very delightful and graciously responded to many questions presented by our students. She thanked the audience for the high-quality questions asked by our students and told them that they were well on their way to being successful authors.

Our faculty was fortunate to hear a comprehensive, sincere, and very practical presentation by our district's chief financial officer. He was invited to our staff development morning for the prime purpose of introducing himself to our staff. As a by-product of his visit, he discussed the proposed bond and answered questions posed by teachers. He was well received, with great compliments about his easy manner, genuine personality, and knowledge.

Third-, fourth-, and fifth-grade teachers continue staff development with our guest lecturer. This month's focus is on scoring children's work using rubrics.

Thanksgiving feasts of all kinds were experienced throughout the school. These feasts ranged from full meals from soup to nuts, to simple apple pie baking, to elaborate ethnic feasts in which children from 18 countries brought in samples of their native foods. Parents, too, enjoyed many of the celebrations.

Finally, attached to this memo is next month's events. As usual, please look this over for your own scheduling needs. A reminder: Please remember to mark the calendar in the main office for any event (field trips, class visitors, etc.) that may warrant notice to the entire school. Our main calendar is a great source of information for each of us. Thanks for your help, as always!

Resource F
Parents' Elementary School Guidebook

Dear Parents/Guardians,

As always, you are cordially welcomed to our school. The word *our* truly means our children, our parents, our teachers, and our entire staff. Together, we enable our school to climb to its greatest heights. Please become as involved as possible in your child(ren)'s education. We need you and your valuable input. So many exciting programs have come directly from you, our parents. Do use this "Parents' Elementary School Guidebook," as it contains important information about our school. Also, should you have any concerns, questions, or ideas, feel free to call me. As indicated in the guidebook, I try to be available each morning from 8:45 to 9:15 a.m. for your calls. However, should this time not be convenient for you, please call any time. I'll get back to you as soon as possible. In closing, may I wish you and your family a very successful year.

Sincerely,

Your Elementary School Principal

Academically Gifted Program

Children are chosen on a districtwide, competitive basis. All eligible district elementary school students (including parochial schools) are put into a pool; academic scores, teacher recommendation, and results of a school case conference are all weighed for final results. Students in Grades 3, 4, and 5 who are selected for the program will be notified in writing by the district director of the Academically Gifted Program.

These classes meet at our school during the following times:

Third grade: Wednesday, 9:00 to 11:00 a.m.

Fourth grade: Thursday, 9:00 to 11:00 a.m.

Fifth grade: Tuesday, 9:00 to 11:00 a.m.

Attendance, Absence, Lateness

Every child is urged to form excellent habits regarding attendance and promptness. A right start every day helps foster a positive attitude. Should your child be absent, please call the school office after 7:00 a.m. Should you fail to report the absence or lateness, our school nurse will call you. This is a practice we've instituted to ensure the safe arrival of our children.

Note: State law requires a note from the parent giving the reason for the child's absence. This note must accompany your child upon his or her return to school. Children should arrive before 8:23 a.m. (the start of the school day) and should assemble at their designated areas.

Block Scheduling

Grades 2, 3, 4, and 5 use a management system developed for the primary purposes of:

1. Eliminating as many pullouts as possible
2. Maximizing the direct instruction of both the classroom teacher and the specialists

Parallel block scheduling gives teachers blocks of uninterrupted time for instruction. While one group of students remains with the classroom teacher for directed instruction, the other group of students moves out of the classroom to an extension center, where they receive enrichment in the curriculum concepts. Students in need of support services proceed to their special service during the extension time, and although they miss extension classes, they are truly being helped in their areas of special need. Therefore, no child ever misses the direct instruction of reading or math taught by the classroom teacher. The concept has met with great success according to students, teachers, and parents alike. The first grade will use the block scheduling concept with a different approach. There will be blocks of uninterrupted directed instructional time, but children will not move to an extension center. It is felt that this use of time is better suited to first-grade work.

Breakfast Program

Breakfast will be available to our children. All are invited to participate from 7:45 a.m. to 8:15 a.m. at a cost of $1.00. Students eligible for free lunch are also entitled to a free breakfast. The same form used for free lunch will be applied to this program.

Bus Transportation

Prekindergartners, kindergartners, first graders, and second graders who live more than half a mile from school are eligible for bus transportation. Should you wish to pick up your child or to have him or her walk home, you must write a note to the teacher stating this request. No exceptions will be made, because any deviation might cause a serious mix-up or might cause the child to become confused and upset.

Conduct

Each student is expected to act in a responsible manner in order to gain the fullest benefits of his or her educational experiences. It is expected that a student should work to the best of his or her ability in all academic, cocurricular, and extracurricular pursuits and strive toward the highest level of achievement possible; that he or she should contribute to an orderly, learning-centered environment; that he or she should show due respect for other persons and for property; and that he or she should seek help in solving problems. To assist in this area, one excellent alternative is offered to our students, namely, conflict resolution.

Conflict Resolution

In an effort to assist children to resolve their problems in an appropriate, effective manner, a program of conflict resolution has been established. Many teachers and approximately 25 fifth graders are trained as "conflict managers." This team of students helps peers who are experiencing difficulties. Children are asked by an adult member of the staff if they wish to take advantage of going to "mediation" about their problem. Should all parties agree, an appointment is made (always during the students' lunch hour) by one of the moderators of the program. A student team plus a trained adult will be available for a mediation session. The adult is located within reasonable proximity to the student session and is called upon in case of an urgent need that may not be settled appropriately by the students.

Consultation Time—Daily

To encourage excellent communication between home and school, I urge you to feel free to call me during my daily consultation time of 8:45 to 9:15 a.m. to ask any question you might have. Your concerns are our concerns. Just remember, if you have a question, no matter what it is, call "the source," and I hope I will be able to answer it. If not, I'll be sure to find the answer for you.

Dining Room

Proper dining room behavior is expected from each child. Teachers and teacher aides in charge help ensure that children are sitting while eating, that they are socializing in an appropriate manner with their friends, and that they eat their whole lunch. We ask that snacks be as nutritious as possible. Part of what we learn about in health classes teaches about the benefits of eating nutritious foods, so you can help in this regard.

We emphasize the following rules:

> No running around
>
> No shouting
>
> No throwing food

All children eat in the dining room, and no one is permitted to leave the premises during the lunch hour. Should you wish special permission, please notify us in writing, because we take our responsibility very seriously in this regard.

The cost of a school lunch, which includes milk, is $1.25. Of course, children may bring lunch from home and may purchase milk if they wish for 30 cents. Free and reduced-price lunches are provided to qualified children. Forms are sent home from the main office concerning those in need of this service.

Lunch periods are held according to the following schedule:

11:20 to 11:50:	Grade 1 eats in dining room.
11:55 to 12:25:	Grades 1, 2, and 3 have recess.
	Grades 4 and 5 eat in dining room.
12:25 to 12:55:	Grades 2 and 3 eat in dining room.
	Grades 4 and 5 have recess.

Directors

Fortunately, in our district there is a K-12 director for each of the curriculum areas. These knowledgeable men and women assist in curriculum development and implementation. District directors are available in the following areas:

Academically Gifted Program

Compensatory Education and Support Service

English/Language Arts

Evaluation and Computer Technology

Guidance

Health, Physical Education, and Athletics

Mathematics

Occupational Education

Performing and Fine Arts

Science

Social Studies

Special Education

Drills

Our school conducts drills for the purpose of order and safety in the event of an emergency.

There are three types of drills about which you should be aware:

Fire Drills. Fire drills are conducted several times a year so that children may practice quick and efficient exits from the school.

Emergency Drills. Emergency drills are used in the event of a weather catastrophe (hurricane, tornado, etc.) or other such emergency in which it might be safer to remain in school rather than to send children home.

Go-Home Drill. A go-home drill would be put into effect in the case of an extreme area emergency (railroad, air disaster, etc.) that might cause roads to be closed or telephone wires to be down. You are urged to talk to your child(ren) about where to go in case you are not home at a particular time. This plan should be routinely discussed periodically so that everyone knows what to do in such an emergency. The district will notify all local radio stations should an extreme emergency arise that would cause the district to decide to dismiss children early. We will also make every effort to contact class captains to immediately begin a parental notification phone chain.

Health and Medical Services

Should a child become ill or injured in school, it is essential that he or she proceed immediately to the health office. No one who has been injured or has become ill during the school day should ever leave school without going to the office for an official sign-out. If it becomes necessary for a child to be sent home, the parent or guardian will be contacted and informed of this fact. No child is ever sent home unless there is an authorized adult to care for him or her. An emergency telephone number is absolutely necessary in such situations. In fact, state law demands that the school have this emergency telephone number on file.

Health certificates are required by state law for each pupil upon entrance to school. Furthermore, children entering first, third, seventh, and tenth grades are required to furnish such documentation. If you do not submit proof of the appropriate examinations by your own physician by early October for children in Grades 1 and 3, it will be assumed that the school doctor will make the examination. Children are routinely given vision, hearing, and scoliosis tests by the school nurse. They are also routinely checked for head lice during the first few days of school. If the nurse's screening indicates a possible problem, the parent or guardian will be notified immediately.

Homework Policy

As defined by the regulations of the board of education,

Homework is studying at home and is ordinarily an extension of classroom instruction.

The purpose of homework is the improvement of the learning process by reinforcing newly acquired skills, by engaging in preparatory activities such as in reading for background, and by extending and applying classroom learning for developing new and deeper understanding.

Homework should be assigned regularly to all pupils and should progressively increase in amount from the primary grades through the high school.

Teachers should ensure that assignments are made that are necessary and useful, appropriate to the ability and maturity level of students, well explained and motivating, and clearly understood by students and, where appropriate, by parents. Guidelines should be provided regarding how the homework assignment might be approached. Because any assignment that is worth making is worth evaluation, teachers should monitor homework carefully and provide pupils the feedback needed to enhance learning.

Principals should take steps to prepare and communicate procedures for homework and to coordinate homework assignments so that pupils are not, for example, overloaded when they have long and difficult assignments one night and have little or no homework the next, or when they return from an extended absence during which an overburdening amount of homework has accumulated.

Parents should be aware that homework assignments ordinarily indicate what pupils have been doing in school and should provide encouragement to strengthen the link between home and school.

Suggestion: Should illness prevent your child from attending school, it is strongly recommended that you not ask your child's teacher for homework. The rationale stems directly from the board's regulations that "homework assignments ordinarily indicate what pupils have been doing in school"! When your child is absent, he or she is missing that valuable firsthand teaching experience and therefore may become frustrated with work with which he or she is unfamiliar. Therefore, when your child returns to school, the teacher will make every effort to provide the necessary guidance to close the learning gap.

As a practical rule: When sick, your child's assignment is to get better!

Inclement Weather

In the event of inclement weather, children will assemble in the following areas:

Pre-K in their assigned classrooms

Kindergarten in Hall 1

Grades 1, 2, and 3 in main lobby

Grades 4 and 5 in Hall 2

Lost and Found

Please try to sew name tags into sweaters, jackets, gloves, hats, and so forth. In addition, boots, sneakers, school bags, and lunch boxes should be clearly marked with your child's name. Identification should always appear in pocketbooks, wallets, and schoolbooks, too.

Inquiries concerning lost items should be made in the main office.

Opportunities and Services Offered

Our school and district offer a wide range of activities and services both in and out of class to broaden the horizons of our pupils. Here are some examples:

Academically Gifted Program

After-School Classes (sponsored by PTA)

Band

Chorus

Computer Education

Conflict Resolution (managed by students with adult supervision)

Contests (Spelling Bees, Essay, Art, Poetry, etc.)

Families Read Every Day (FRED)

Intramurals (before and after school)

Math Olympiads

Occupational therapy for approved students

Orchestra

Parents as Reading Partners (PARP; sponsored by PTA)

Remedial reading services for approved students

Resource room services for approved students

Safety Patrol, a fifth-grade activity

Speech services for approved students

Student Council

Summer Reading Program

Yearbook Committee

Portfolio/Authentic Assessment

Our kindergartners and first graders will continue with this concept, which we believe provides a visual documentation of what your child is learning. Both your child and his or her teacher will choose pieces of work that demonstrate how your child has progressed from one stage to the next. During conference times, you will have the opportunity to review these pieces of work and to discuss what you see with the teacher and come to some joint understandings of your child's progress. You will be notified, as usual, of your scheduled conference time. We believe that much will be gained from these exchanges, so please make every effort to be present. It is very, very important to your child.

Safety

At school, we caution children about the dangers of crossing in the middle of a street. This is especially true in front of our school. Please do not fall victim to the temptation to save a few seconds and risk injury. Cross at the corner, not in between.

Cars are not permitted in the parking lot for purposes of picking up or dropping off children. This is a dangerous practice. We need everyone's cooperation to avoid this dangerous situation.

Walking through the parking lot is not permitted. Please use the entry on the Main Road and walk on the grassy area. Should wheeling a stroller or carriage through the grass be difficult, we urge you to walk to the front of the building, spend the extra few moments, and be on the safe side.

Should a person other than yourself be picking up your child(ren), please notify the teacher in writing. This safety measure is one about which we are very strict for obvious reasons.

If you are picking up a child because of illness or an early appointment, you are required to come into the main office to officially sign out the child.

School Records

Please feel free to review your child's academic records on a regular basis. Give our secretary a call to arrange a mutually agreeable time to come in to review the records. Your questions will always be addressed, and I'll walk you through the contents of your child's cumulative folder if you like.

Shared-Decision-Making/ Site-Based Management Team

A *site-based team* is defined as "an organizational strategy for the participation of parents, community representatives, teachers, other members of a school's staff and administration, and sometimes students; it decentralizes authority and the decision-making process."

The plan for our district has been developed by a committee of teachers, parents, and administrators with the approval of the board of education in compliance with the Commissioner's Regulation.

The plan includes seven parts:

1. The educational issues that will be subject to shared decision making

2. The manner and extent of involvement of all parties

3. The means for assessing improved student performance

4. The ways in which the building committees will be accountable for their decisions

5. A dispute resolution process

6. The manner in which existing state and federal regulations for parent involvement will be coordinated in the plan

7. The training in the shared-decision-making process

There are 11 members on our school's site-based team: 4 teachers, 4 parents, 1 district director with elementary school responsibilities, 1 community member, and the principal.

Our team meets at least monthly, with notices of meetings posted for your convenience on the bulletin board outside the main office. All are invited to come, observe, and give your ideas to any member of the team.

Snacks

Because learning about nutritious food is part of our curriculum, we urge you to think about snacks very seriously. Candy, foods with a lot of sugar, and so forth are often poor health choices. As you already know, some children prefer junk food over a nutritious lunch. Therefore, we ask you to help in the teaching process by stressing to your child that a snack is not a substitute for good food.

Test Policy

For your information, a schedule of tests administered to our children is included in the district calendar. You will also receive a school flier prior to the administration of standardized testing to inform you of the testing dates. Parents/guardians will receive results of California Achievement Testing as soon as they become available from the testing service. Of course, you are welcome to come in for an explanation of these results should you wish further clarification. Call the office or speak with your child's teacher, and we'll be happy to schedule an appointment at a mutually convenient time.

Our students take the following tests:

Grades 2 through 5, California Achievement Tests

Grade 3, Cognitive Ability Test

Grade 4, Program Evaluation Test in Science, Pupil Evaluation Program (PEP) in Language Arts and Math

Grade 5, California Achievement Tests plus the PEP test in Writing

Textbooks

Each child is responsible for textbooks that are distributed to him or her. Books should be covered, labeled with name and class, and properly cared for. Should loss or damage occur, either cost of replacement or a reasonable fee will be expected.

Vandalism

In order to maintain the beauty and safety of our school, it is important for you to know that both the board of education and the school administration take a strong position regarding prosecution of known vandals. Official police complaints will be signed where known violators have been identified and previously warned. We look to you and your usual cooperation to help keep our school beautiful and safe day and night. To this end, we will notify the police department whenever evening activities are scheduled so that they can schedule officers to assist in supervising the area.

Visitor's Rose

When visiting your school, helping out in a class, or attending a meeting with a teacher, you are required to come to the main office first to receive a rose. As a safety measure, the rose identifies you as a welcomed visitor. Please cooperate in this regard. Teachers are cooperating in this regard, too, as they will ask any visitor, known to them or not, to please go to the main office for a rose.

A televised monitoring system has been installed in our elementary school. The system includes cameras and televised monitors in the main office as an additional safety measure.

Although we caution children about interacting with strangers in matters such as taking rides or answering specific questions about themselves (this includes family friends, unless parents give permission), we need your assistance in reinforcing this concept at home. Perhaps you'll consider a code word known only to your family. In this way, your child will know that the message is coming directly from home.

Parents Can Make the Difference

Parents can help their children reach their full potential in school. The home environment and the quality and quantity of time spent with your child(ren) can make the difference. Here are some ideas:

Provide a suitable space for study and work.

Praise your child for the work shown to you.

Help your child organize his or her work.

Help your child to be responsible for coming to school prepared.

Set reasonable standards of behavior, and help your child meet them.

Communicate your problems or concerns to the teacher or principal.

Participate in school-sponsored activities with your child.

Make sure your child gets healthy meals, enough sleep, and good exercise.

Avoid comparing your child to brothers, sisters, and friends.

Limit and monitor the television programs watched by your child(ren).

Encourage reading! Help your child find worthwhile reading materials.

If your child is home ill, his or her homework should be to get well. Teachers will take care of makeup work, if necessary, upon your child's return to school. If your child insists on doing something academic, try reading a book. He or she could read a part, and you could add to the interest by reading a part, too.

Many thanks for your cooperation, interest, and involvement. We look forward to seeing you often throughout the coming year. We wish you and your family a most successful year. Together, we can make it all happen!

Resource G
Best Practices in
Quality Education for Students
With Severe Disabilities

Inclusion

Students with disabilities are welcomed into their communities, schools, and regular education classrooms. Students attend their home schools (the schools they would attend if they did not have a disability) and access the total school environment.

Functional Curriculum

Students are taught clusters of skills and activities that have direct practical applications within their daily lives. Age-appropriateness: Materials, activities, and interactions are appropriate to students' chronological ages (not so-called mental ages).

Individually Adapted
Curriculum and Instruction

Curriculum, instruction, and support strategies are designed to meet the individual needs of each student. All necessary modifications to meet students' programmatic or support needs are provided within inclusive school and community environments.

192

Community-Referenced Instruction

As students get older, they are provided instruction in recreation and leisure, domestic and home living, general community functioning, and vocational environments within the school and community.

Home-School Collaboration

School and family practice a team approach to the educational process. Parents are involved as active and visible participants in decision making throughout the school years.

Circles of Friendship and Support

Students experience the support network of peers. They need to be included within their classrooms, schools, and communities. When necessary, teams of adults and children work together to problem-solve how students with disabilities can be fully included.

Integrated Therapy for Related Services

Related services (e.g., speech/language, physical therapy, and occupational therapy) support students' participation in school and community environments. Educational and therapeutic techniques are cooperatively designed to assess, plan, implement, evaluate, and report progress on educational needs and goals. Therapists provide both direct service to students and indirect consultative services to other educators.

Positive Approaches to Challenging Behavior

Nonaversive interventions are used to address behavior problems. The purposes or functions of a problem behavior are identified, and team members problem-solve and design strategies for (a) preventing the behavior, (b) teaching alternative desirable skills to meet this function or purpose, and (c) reacting appropriately if the behavior does occur.

Resource H
Teacher Job Description

Goal of the Position

The goal is to ensure that all students for whom the teacher is responsible demonstrate educational, personal, and career growth through a thorough and efficient program of teaching and learning that is consistent with the Code of Ethics of the Education Profession; with the district's philosophy, goals, and objectives; and with individual student activities.

Major Performance Objectives

1. To plan instruction

2. To conduct instruction toward the achievement of pupil performance objectives and the goals and objectives of district and building programs

3. To develop a climate that encourages a positive self-concept in each student

4. To evaluate the progress of pupils toward pupil performance objectives and the goals and objectives of district and building programs

5. To manage the routines and duties of the position in compliance with federal and state laws, district policies, and the regulations of the district and the school

6. To maintain and improve school-community relations

7. To evidence personal and professional development

Major Responsibilities

1.1. Lists the essential and desirable goals and performance objectives for pupils together with the process skills in unit plans

1.2. Identifies strategies for group-based instruction and other grouping practices

1.3. Determines procedures for assessing entry-level skills of pupils at the beginning of a unit, mastery-level skills after instruction for determining alternative prescriptions, and achievement of end-of-unit goals and objectives

1.4. Selects and develops materials and activities designed to reach the objectives

1.5. Determines homework assignments relevant to the objectives

1.6. Cooperates with others in planning for instruction and special programs

1.7. Utilizes principles of learning psychology in planning

1.8. Follows the curricular guides and courses of study prescribed by the board

2.1. Informs pupils of the objectives of instruction and works toward them

2.2. Uses a variety of methods, materials, supplies, equipment, outside resources, and so forth to make class work interesting

2.3. Utilizes a range of activities, time, and materials appropriate for mastery

2.4. Presents and explains materials in a well-organized fashion to use class time efficiently

2.5. Assigns and follows up homework relevant to the objectives

2.6. Discriminates among learning styles of pupils

3.1. Is sensitive to pupil's abilities, interests, feelings, values, and aspirations

3.2. Respects pupils as human beings, regardless of performance

3.3. Encourages pupils to develop a realistic self-concept as well as self-initiation, self-direction, and self-evaluation skills

3.4. Encourages and develops a desire to learn by providing opportunities for success

3.5. Helps pupils anticipate and cope with the uncertain and changing future

3.6. Develops and maintains student morale

4.1. Makes preassessments of pupil entry levels for instruction

4.2. Prepares tests that are directly relevant to goals and objectives

4.3. Compares student achievement to prespecified objectives of instruction and relates these to the district's promotional policies

4.4. Provides pupils with continuous and timely knowledge of results

4.5. Understands the purposes and meaning of standardized tests, cooperates in their administration, and uses the results in redirecting instruction

5.1. Maintains discipline and good order in classrooms and elsewhere throughout the building

5.2. Supervises assistants (aides, student teachers, etc.)

5.3. Is available for conducting conferences and reporting progress to parents in an effective manner

5.4. Prepares such records, reports, and requisitions as the superintendent, the principal, or their designees may require

5.5. Administers and enforces the policies and regulations of the district

5.6. Performs such other duties as are customarily conducted by instructional personnel as assigned by the superintendent, the principal, or their designees

5.7. Supervises student activity in a variety of locations such as classrooms, libraries, cafeterias, and so forth

6.1. Communicates effectively with pupils and parents

6.2. Uses precise and supportive criticism so that students respond constructively

6.3. Is fair, objective, and impartial in treatment of pupils

6.4. Participates in decision making on various levels

7.1. Is familiar with and observes district and building policies and regulations

7.2. Meets attendance and punctuality requirements

7.3. Works cooperatively with colleagues and the administration

7.4. Accepts critiquing and supervision in striving for improvement

7.5. Keeps abreast of new developments related to his or her teaching assignment

7.6. Participates in curriculum development and shows a willingness to seek and implement promising ideas

7.7. Evaluates his or her instruction realistically and seriously tries to meet professional goals

Resource I
Helping Children Cope at Holiday Time

Dear Parent/Guardian,

"Banana Splits" groups for children whose parents have been separated or divorced are being formed. The time span is not important—children will benefit if their parents are recently separated or if their parents have been divorced for many years.

This program is designed to help make the transition easier, to assist children in accepting difficult changes and help them to realize other children are in similar situations, and to improve academic and social functioning. We will use age-appropriate activities, discussions, and resources with an emphasis on open and honest sharing, fun, friendship, and confidentiality.

Sessions are approximately 45 minutes long and will be held at a time that will not be disruptive to the academic program (usually during lunch and recess). Children will usually be grouped according to age/grade.

If you would like your child to be involved in this rewarding experience, please return the attached permission slip to school as soon as possible. If you have any questions related to this activity, please call the principal's office.

Sincerely,

Your Elementary School Principal

- -

I would like my child to participate in the Banana Splits program. I understand the guidelines of strictest confidence will apply for all group activities.

_____

Parent Signature

_____   _____

Home Telephone   Work Telephone

_____   _____

Your Child's Name   Your Child's Teacher's Name

_____

Comments

Resource J
Request for Retirement
Congratulatory Letter

The President
The White House
Washington, D.C. 20500

Dear Mr. President:

The faculty and staff of the Our Elementary School are honoring our secretary, Ms. Mackay, on the occasion of her retirement on Wednesday, June 2. Ms. Mackay has been an active member of our school district for over 25 years. As secretary of the Our Elementary School, she has served the students, staff, and parents in a variety of ways. Her sense of humor, her dedication to the members of the community, her skill in keeping everyone "on track," and her knowledge of the myriad details involved in the everyday operations of our school are worthy of distinguished honor.

We would be grateful for an acknowledgment from you, because Ms. Mackay has been an outstanding secretary and has brought a great sense of commitment to her position.

With grateful appreciation,

The Principal

Resource K
Attention Deficit Disorder

Suggested Classroom Accommodations for Specific Behaviors

Although the information provided below is designed to be used with students with Attention Deficit Disorder, much of it is useful for students with a wide range of learning disabilities. Prepared by the ADHD Task Force of the Anchorage, Alaska, School District.

When You See This Behavior	*Try This Accommodation*
1. Difficulty following a plan with high aspirations, lack of follow-through; sets out to "get straight *As*, ends up with *Fs*" (i.e., sets unrealistic goals)	Assist student in setting long-range goals; break the goal into realistic parts. Use a questioning strategy with the student. Ask, "What do you need to be able to do this?" Keep asking that question until the student has reached an obtainable goal. Have student set clear timelines for what he needs to do to accomplish each step. (Monitor student's progress frequently.)
2. Difficulty sequencing and completing steps to accomplish specific tasks such as writing a book report or term paper, organizing paragraphs, doing division problem, and so forth	Break up task into workable and obtainable steps. Provide examples and specific steps to accomplish the task.
*3. Shifting from one uncompleted activity to another without closure	Define the requirements of a completed activity. For example, "Your math is finished when all six problems are complete and correct; do not begin on the next task until it is finished."
*4. Difficulty following through on instructions from others	Gain student's attention before giving directions. Use alerting cues. Accompany oral directions with written directions. Give one direction at a time. Quietly repeat directions to the student after they have been given to the rest of the class. Check for understanding by having the student repeat the directions. Place general methods of operation and expectations on charts displayed around the room or on sheets to be included in student's notebook.

When You See This Behavior	*Try This Accommodation*
5. Difficulty prioritizing from the most to least important	Prioritize assignments and activities. Provide a model to help the student. Post the model and refer to it often.
6. Difficulty sustaining effort and accuracy over time	Reduce assignment length and strive for quality rather than quantity. Increase the frequency of positive reinforcements. Catch the student doing it right and let him or her know it.
7. Difficulty completing assignments	List or post (and say) all steps necessary to complete each assignment. Reduce the assignment into manageable sections with specific due dates. Make frequent checks for work and assignment completion. Arrange for the student to have a "study buddy" available in each subject area.
8. Difficulty with any task that requires memory	Combine seeing, saying, writing, and doing; student may need to subvocalize to remember. Teach memory techniques as a study strategy (e.g., mnemonics, visualization, oral rehearsal, numerous repetitions).
9. Difficulty with test taking	Allow extra time for testing, teach test-taking skills and strategies, and allow student to be tested orally. Use clear, readable, and uncluttered test forms. Use test format that the student is most comfortable with. Allow sample spaces for student response. Consider having lined answer spaces for essay or short-answer tests.
10. Confusion from nonverbal cues (misreads body language, etc.)	Directly teach (tell the student) what nonverbal cues mean. Model and have student practice reading cues in a safe setting.
11. Confusion from written material, for example, difficulty finding the main idea of a paragraph, tendency to attribute greater importance to minor details	Provide student with a copy of reading material with main ideas underlined or highlighted. Provide an outline of important points from reading material. Teach outlining and main idea/details concepts. Provide tape of text or chapter.
12. Confusion from spoken material, lectures, and audiovisual material, for example, difficulty finding main ideas from presentation, tendency to attribute greater importance to minor details	Provide student with a copy of presentation notes. Allow peers to share notes from presentation. Have student compare own notes with copy of peer's notes. Provide framed outlines of presentations, introducing visual and auditory cues to important information.
*13. Difficulty sustaining attention to tasks or other activities; easily distracted by extraneous stimuli	Reward attention. Break up activities into small units. Reward for timely accomplishments. Use physical proximity and touch. Use earphones or study carrels, quiet place, or preferential seating.

When You See This Behavior	*Try This Accommodation*
*14. Frequent messiness or sloppiness	Teach organizational skills. Be sure student has daily, weekly, and monthly assignment sheets; list of materials needed daily; and consistent format for papers. Have a consistent way for students to turn in and receive back papers. Reduce distractions. Give reward points for notebook checks and proper paper format. Provide clear copies of worksheets and handouts and consistent format for worksheets. Establish a daily routine, and provide models for what you want the students to do. Arrange for a peer who will help with organization. Assist student to keep materials in a specific place, such as pencils in pouch. Be willing to repeat expectations.
15. Poor handwriting (often mixing cursive with manuscript and capitals with lowercase letters)	Allow for a scribe, and grade for content, not handwriting. Allow for use of a computer or typewriter. Consider alternative methods for student responses, such as tape recorder, oral reports, and so forth. Don't penalize student for mixing cursive and manuscript. Accept any method of production.
16. Difficulty with fluency in handwriting, for example, good letter and word production, but very slow and laborious	Allow for shorter assignments (quality vs. quantity). Allow alternate method of production (computer, scribe, oral presentation, etc.).
17. Poorly developed study skills	Teach study skills specific to the subject areas of organization (e.g., assignment calendar), textbook reading, note taking (finding main ideas/details, mapping, outlining, skimming, summarizing).
18. Poor self-monitoring, such as careless errors in arithmetic, spelling, and reading	Teach specific methods of self-monitoring, such as "stop-look-listen." Have student proofread finished work after a day or two.
19. Low fluency or production of written material (takes hours on a 10-minute assignment)	Allow for alternative method for completing assignment (oral presentation, taped report, visual presentation, graphs, maps, pictures, etc.) with reduced written requirements. Allow for alternative method of writing, such as typewriter, computer, cursive or printing, or a scribe.
*20. Apparent inattention (underactive daydreaming, "not here")	Get student's attention before giving directions. Tell the student how to pay attention: "Look at me when I talk," "Watch my eyes when I speak." Ask student to repeat directions. Attempt to actively involve student in lesson, for example, by cooperative learning.

When You See This Behavior	*Try This Accommodation*
*21. Difficulty participating in class without being interruptive; difficulty working quietly	Seat student in close proximity to the teacher. Reward appropriate behavior; catch student "being good." Use study carrel if appropriate.
22. Inappropriate seeking of attention: clowns around; exhibits loud, excessive, or exaggerated movements as attention-seeking behavior; interrupts; butts in to other children's activities; needles others	Show student (model) how to gain others' attention appropriately. Catch the student behaving appropriately and reinforce.
*23. Frequent, excessive talking	Use hand signals to prompt student behavior about when and when not to talk. Make sure student is called when it is appropriate, and reinforce listening.
24. Difficulty making transitions (from activity to activity or class to class); for example, takes an excessive amount of time to find pencil, gives up, refuses to leave previous task, appears agitated during change	Program child for transitions. Give advance warning when a transition is going to take place: "Now we are completing the worksheet; next we will . . ." and clarify the expectations for the transition: "and you will need . . ." Specifically assemble and display lists of materials needed until a routine is possible. List steps necessary to complete each assignment. Have specific locations for all materials, such as pencil pouches, tabs in notebooks, and so forth. Arrange for an organized helper (peer).
25. Difficulty remaining seated or in a particular position when required to	Give student frequent opportunities to get up and move around. Allow space for movement.
26. Frequent fidgeting with hands, feet, or objects; squirming in seat	Break tasks down into small increments, and give frequent positive reinforcement for accomplishments, as this type of behavior is often due to frustration. Allow alternative movement when possible.
27. Inappropriate responses in class often blurted out; answers given to questions before they have been completed	Seat student in close proximity to teacher so that visual and physical monitoring of student behavior can be done by the teacher. State behavior that you want. Tell the student how you expect him or her to behave.
28. Agitation under pressure and competition (academic or athletic)	Stress effort and enjoyment for self, rather than competition with others. Minimize timed activities, and structure class for team effort and cooperation.
29. Inappropriate behaviors in a team or large-group sport or athletic activity; difficulty waiting for turn in games or group situations	Give the student a responsible job (e.g., class captain, care and distributing of the balls, score keeping, etc.); consider leadership role. Have the student in close proximity to teacher.

When You See This Behavior	Try This Accommodation
30. Frequent involvement with physically dangerous activities without considering possible consequences	Anticipate dangerous situations and plan for in advance. Stress stop-look-listen. Pair with responsible peer. Rotate responsible students so they don't wear out.
31. Poor adult interactions; defies authority	Provide positive attention. Talk with student about the inappropriate behavior: "What you are doing is . . ." Suggest alternative methods: "A better way of getting what you want is . . ."
32. Frequent self-putdowns, poor personal care and posture, negative comments about self and others, poor self-esteem	Structure for success. Train student for self-monitoring, reinforce improvements, and teach self-questioning strategies (What am I doing? How is that going to affect others?). Allow opportunities for the student to show his or her strength. Give positive recognition.
33. Difficulty using unstructured time in special places, such as recess, hallways, lunchroom, locker room, library, assembly	Provide student with a definite purpose during unstructured activities: "The purpose of going to the library is to check out books." Encourage group games and participation, such as organized school clubs and activities.
*34. Losing things necessary for task or activities at school or at home, such as pencils, books, and assignments before, during, and after completion of a given task	Help student organize. Frequently monitor notebook and dividers, pencil, pouch, locker, book bag, and desks. Provide positive reinforcement for good organization. Provide student with a list of needed materials and their locations.
35. Poor use of time, for example, sitting, staring off into space, doodling, not working on task at hand	Teach reminder cues, such as a gentle touch on the shoulder, hand signals, and so forth. Tell the student your expectations of what paying attention looks like: "You look like you are paying attention when . . ." Give the student a time limit for a small unit of work, with positive reinforcement for accurate completion. Use contract, timer, and so forth for self-monitoring.

Note: An asterisk indicates the most dominant behaviors displayed by students with attention deficit disorder.

Resource L
Parallel Block Scheduling

Dear Parents/Guardians,

I hope this letter finds you and your family in the best of health and enjoying the hot weather. Some of you have heard about the time management approach we will be using in our second grade this fall, called "parallel block scheduling." (Grades 3, 4, and 5 have been successfully using this system for several years.)

Here is some background on the concept: During the past decade, federal, state, and local boards of education have implemented many programs directed at meeting the needs of specific portions of the student population. The result has been a myriad of worthwhile educational programs that have been labeled *pull-outs*. The programs have been identified by this term, because they pull students out from the regular classroom during instructional time periods. Our elementary classroom teachers and children feel the greatest impact from pullout programs. When children go to or come from a support service, it sometimes causes interruption of class instruction. This situation sometimes causes frustration for the classroom teacher, who wants to maximize the learning experience for every child in the class, for the child, who does not wish to miss material presented while he or she is out of the room, and for the teacher of the pullout program, who feels that he or she is actually in competition for an individual student's available instructional time.

The concept of parallel block scheduling eliminates this situation. The idea has been successfully used by hundreds of schools throughout the country, and our school joins in that success. Here is how it works. Each homeroom class is divided into two groups for direct instruction in reading and math. While half the group is instructed in reading, the second half moves out of the homeroom and either goes for reading enrichment to an "extension class" or proceeds to a support service such as speech, the resource room, and so forth if appropriate. The same procedure is followed during the math instructional time. After the scheduled period is over, children from the extension class (or support service) return to the homeroom for teacher-directed instruction, and the other group goes to extension or support service. In other words, the two groups exchange places. Because instruction occurs in both the extension class and in the homeroom, the amount of teacher-directed instruction is increased significantly. Most important, there is no movement from students being pulled out for special services during direct instruction times.

The beauty of the concept is primarily that the homeroom teacher's time is strictly devoted to teaching the small group that is in his or her class at the time. The teacher no longer needs to provide independent work for those children with whom he or she is not working. Instead, they will be attending the extension class or receiving support services. If no services are required, then the child will be provided enrichment instruction, the kind of instruction that is not imperative to learning a particular skill.

Extension classes become arenas where activities extend and enhance instruction that began in the homeroom class. Literature appreciation, problem solving, hands-on activities, application to authentic situations, and emphasis on the higher-order thinking skills (categorizing, synthesizing, comparing and contrasting, etc.) are just some of the types of instruction that are appropriate in extension classes. Such use of school time has been viewed as superior to the organization of the day as we once knew it.

Finally, the rest of the day is generally spent as an entire group. Children attend their special classes such as music, art, physical education, and library as a whole group. Instruction that profits from whole-group interaction, such as science, social studies, and so forth, will occur in the homeroom with almost no interruption at all.

I hope this description will help you understand the design of your child's day in second grade, which features both whole-group activities and small-group instruction. Our aim is always to provide the best for each of our children and to challenge them in every possible way. To date, students, teachers, and parents have been very pleased with the high caliber of results.

Wishing you my best and looking forward to a great new year in September.

Sincerely,

Your Elementary School Principal

Resource M
National TV Turnoff Week

Dear Parents and Students,

The week of April 22 through April 28 is National TV Turnoff Week. This event is sponsored by the American Medical Association plus many other worthy organizations. As research confirms, upon graduation from high school, most children have spent more time watching TV than attending school. Our school is also concerned about these stunning figures. But we are also aware of good time management. So in order to help children understand that TV watching can be an excellent pastime when coupled with other interesting and necessary activities, we will offer an exciting reward for all students who are brave enough to turn off the TV for an entire week. If you, the parent, will verify that there was no more than one hour per day of TV watching by your child(ren) for an entire week, he or she will receive a free ice cream cone from our dining room.

Let's join together in this worthy venture and try to add TV watching to some family games, outdoor play, reading, or other valuable leisure time activity.

Good luck, one and all!

Sincerely,

Your Elementary School Principal

- -

_____   _____
Parent's Name   Child's Name

I certify that my child has not watched TV during the week of April 22 through April 28.

Please return this form to your child's teacher.

Resource N
Standardized Testing Memo to Teachers

Memorandum

To: All Third-Grade Teachers

From: The Principal

Date: February

Re: Standardized Testing Information for Third Grade

As a prelude to next month's standardized tests, here are some guidelines that I hope will serve as a confirmation that you are right on target with your teaching and that your children are "test ready."

Grade 3

Vocabulary

Students should know synonyms, antonyms, prefixes, suffixes, and homonyms.

Comprehension

Students should be able to answer story questions (sequence, inference, main idea, word meanings, prediction).

Language

Students need to know the following:

1. Punctuation, capitalization rules

2. When to end a sentence and start a new one with capital letter

3. Correct letter form (business, friendly)

4. Correct usage (noun-verb agreement: My rabbit only like/likes carrots)

5. Subject and predicate identification

6. How to read two sentences and then choose the sentence that combines both into one sentence

7. How to choose a sentence that best fits into a given story in the correct sequence. For example, "He bought groceries at the store. The food spilled all over the sidewalk."

   (a) The cat ran away.   (b) I had no money.   (c) The bag broke.
   (d) The man smiled.

8. How to find the topic sentence for a given paragraph

9. Given a topic sentence, how to find another sentence that develops the topic sentence

Math Computation

Students should know the following:

   Addition of 2-, 3-, and 4-digit numbers

   Subtraction of 2-, 3-, and 4-digit numbers

   Dollars and cents

   How to multiply by single-digit numbers

   How to divide by single-digit numbers

Math Concepts

Students should know the following:

   What questions you need to ask yourself to determine how to solve a problem

   How to use simple graphs

   How to use Venn diagrams

   How to check a subtraction example

   How to work with pounds and ounces

   The names of solid shapes

   The concept of place value

   How to complete number sequences: 1, 2, 4, 7, __, 11.

   How to tell time

Resource O
Standardized Testing Letter to Parents

Dear Parents/Guardians,

The California Achievement Tests (CAT) will be administered to children in Grades 2 through 5 during the week of March 10. Here are some suggestions for your consideration that will give your child every opportunity to perform to the best of his or her ability:

* It is very important that your child(ren) get to bed at a reasonable hour.

* A healthful breakfast helps test performance.

* Cheerful and encouraging words help put the test in its proper perspective. Although it is wise to recognize the importance of test taking, too much pressure could undermine concentration.

* Number 2 pencils are needed for the test.

* If a child wears glasses, please ensure that they arrive with the child.

CAT test results are anticipated in the late spring, and a copy will be mailed to you. Thanking you for your cooperation.

Sincerely,

Your Elementary School Principal

Resource P
End-of-the-Year Sign-Out Checklist

Name of Teacher: _____ Date: _____

Use this checklist to assist you when you are closing out for the school year.

Items to Be Checked

---

1. _____ Attendance cards and affidavit signed and handed in

2. _____ Permanent record and test cards

3. _____ Report cards completed and distributed

4. _____ Accounts completed

5. _____ Lost books list completed

6. _____ Books on loan from library and office returned

7. _____ Special equipment returned, unless it should be left in class

8. _____ Return of all visual and audio aids

9. _____ Keys returned:

   _____ Classroom

   _____ Cabinet

   _____ Desk

10. _____ All requisitions completed

11. _____   Books for rebinding or discarding stacked and labeled

12. _____   Book inventory complete

13. _____   Class record books completed and filed with principal

Please complete duties listed above that apply to your grade or department.

Summer Address (please print, and include street, town, state, and zip code)

_____

_____

Summer Telephone _____

Principal's Signature for Approval: _____

CORWIN
PRESS

The Corwin Press logo—a raven striding across an open book—represents the happy union of courage and learning. We are a professional-level publisher of books and journals for K–12 educators, and we are committed to creating and providing resources that embody these qualities. Corwin's motto is "Success for All Learners."